EXECUTIVE EDITORS
Sarah Galbraith, Alan Doan, Jenny Doan, David Mifsud

MANAGING EDITOR
Natalie Earnheart

CREATIVE DIRECTOR
Christine Ricks

PHOTOGRAPHER
BPD Studios

CONTRIBUTING PHOTOGRAPHER
Katie Whitt

VIDEOGRAPHER
Jake Doan

DESIGNER & TECHNICAL WRITER
Linda Johnson

PROJECT DESIGN TEAM
Natalie Earnheart, Jenny Doan, Sarah Galbraith

CONTRIBUTING COPY WRITERS
Katie Mifsud, Jenny Doan, Camille Maddox, Natalie Earnheart, Christine Ricks, Alan Doan, Sarah Galbraith, Hillary Sperry

COPY EDITOR
Geoff Openshaw

CONTRIBUTING PIECERS
Jenny Doan, Natalie Earnheart, Stephen Nixdorf, Cassie Nixdorf, Shea Henderson

CONTRIBUTING QUILTERS
Bernice Kelly, Deloris Burnett, Jamey Stone, Kathleen Miller, Betty Bates, Adrian Stacey, Emma Jensen, Sherry Melton, Cassie Martin, Amber Weeks, Sandi Gaunce, Daniela Kirk, Amy Gertz, Patty St. John, Mari Zullig

CONTACT US
Missouri Star Quilt Co
114 N Davis
Hamilton, Mo. 64644
888-571-1122
info@missouriquiltco.com

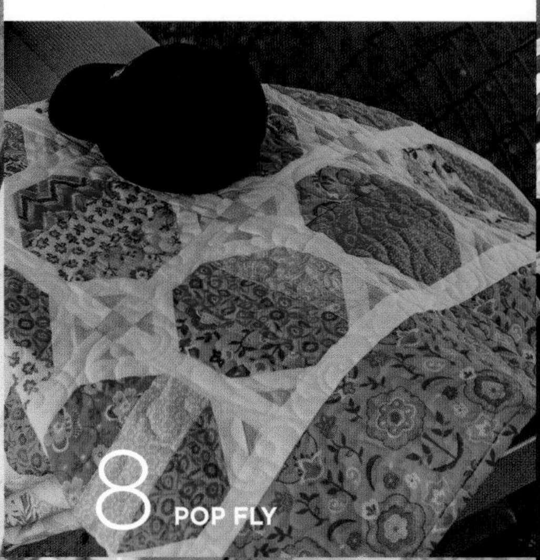

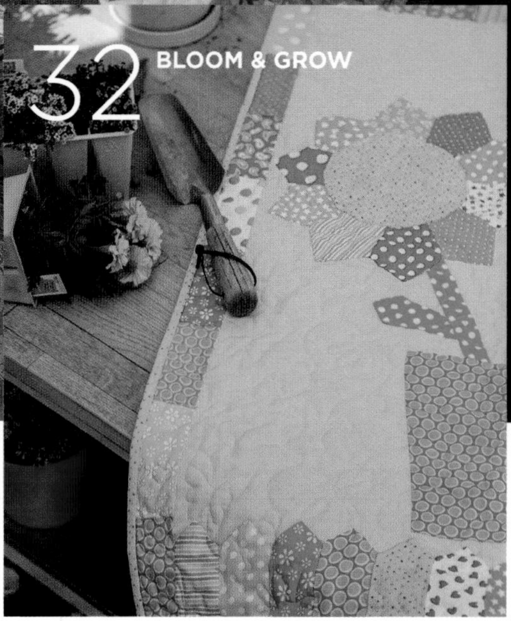

content

HELLO from MSQC

> "We hope our magazine—BLOCK will inspire you to create beautiful quilts."

Don't you just love summer? So many memories come to mind when I think of this wonderful time of year with its long, warm days. There's so much to do: picnics, parades, camping, swimming in the lake, bike rides, and so much more.

I loved having my children out of school for the summer. We often made a big list of all the things we wanted to do over those few months of freedom and would then set off on our little adventures.

The kids particularly loved an excuse to set out on their bikes. Not to be left out, I had a big, three-wheeled bike with a basket on the back. This basket was loaded with a quilt, some lunch, and even children who were too small to ride their own bike! And then we were off to explore!

Summer lends itself to so many spontaneous and wonderful activities. It's as if Mother Nature is begging us to make the most of things, knowing there are colder, shorter days on the horizon.

Of course, the pinnacle of summer is Independence Day. This holiday is filled with so many memories for our family, from designing a family float for the local parade, to picnic lunches, fireman musters, and lying on the grass to watch fireworks at the end of the day. And, of course, many quilts have been involved every step of the way!

As we begin summer, we at the Missouri Star Quilt Company hope you are able to make the most of this wonderful season. Hold hands and go on a walk with your honey! Lay on a quilt and make shapes out of the clouds! Enjoy every moment, because before we know it, the kids are back in school, the windows stay shut, and the long, balmy days of summer are a thing of the past.

Happy Summer!

Jenny

JENNY DOAN
MISSOURI STAR QUILT CO

the dog days of SUMMER are here

I have a friend who LOVES the Fourth of July. It's her favorite holiday. And who doesn't love it, really? It's all about fireworks, parades, great all-american food and gathering as families to celebrate. With its traditional color palette of red, white and blue it's perfect for this month's Color Co-op.

I love this palette of colors. But sometimes I get excited to make it a little less traditional. I can't help but add in some aquas and yellow just to brighten things up and make it extra cheerful. Everything bursts with firecracker color! It's fun to add an unexpected twist.

I hope you enjoy this summer's bundle full of flare. It's a Fourth of July celebration of fabrics from MSQC that guarantees to pop and crackle with creativity. Happy Fourth!

CHRISTINE RICKS
MSQC Creative Director, BLOCK MAGAZINE

SOLIDS

FBY12499 Kona Cotton - Poppy
by Robert Kaufman Fabrics
SKU-K001-1296

FBY12530 Kona Cotton - Surf
by Robert Kaufman Fabrics
SKU-K001-32

FBY12352 Kona Cotton - Bahama Blue
by Robert Kaufman Fabrics
SKU-K001-1011

FBY12498 Kona Cotton - Pool
by Robert Kaufman Fabrics
SKU-K001-45

FBY11287 Citrus - Small Check Yellow
by Another Point of View for Windham Fabrics
SKU-37514-7

FBY3688 Kona Cotton - Ash
by Robert Kaufman Fabrics
SKU-K001-1077

PRINTS

FBY4170 It's A Strike - Star Red/Cream
by Kanvas Studios for Benartex
SKU-0555910B

FBY11074 Serena - Dot Stripe Navy
by Another Point of View for Windham Fabrics
SKU-37383-3

FBY12314 30's Playtime 2014 - 30's Blue
by Chloe's Closet for Moda Fabrics
SKU-32794 12

FBY4352 Small Cotton Chevrons - Aqua
by Riley Blake Designs
SKU-C340-20 AQUA

FBY11287 Citrus - Small Check Yellow
by Another Point of View for Windham Fabrics
SKU-37514-7

FBY8969 Moda Essential Dots - White Baby Blue
by Moda Fabrics
SKU-865461

Play ball!

quilt designed by NATALIE EARNHEART

I believe that the secret to a happy memory is to avoid planning it. Years ago when we got a "new" hand-me-down camera, I became determined to catch our whole family in the perfect, natural, happy moment. I washed the kids' dirty faces, put them in matching outfits, and took them outside. "Play. Have fun," I said. "But a bit slower, the picture will be blurry! And move! You're blocking your sister! And stop messing up your hair! And for heaven's sake get off your brother! No wrestling!"

Long story short, I never got the perfect photo. I got a lot of shots where half the kids looked adorable and the other half were in a blur as they pull their sisters' hair or wrestled a brother to the floor. I also got a whole lot of grouchy kids who hated having their picture taken. (For a while my kids claimed to be allergic to cameras.)

I've learned that you can't choreograph memories. It's during those days when you're just passing the time with the people you love, doing whatever sounds fun, that prized memories are really made.

AL LOVED LITTLE LEAGUE AS A KID, and still enjoys a fun game of baseball with the family!

This strategy served us well, especially when we didn't have much money for activities. In fact, although our kids were nuts about baseball, we could only afford to have one kid on a team at a time. So on lazy days or when the kids were stir-crazy, we grabbed a baseball and headed outside. It didn't matter where, any patch of grass could become a baseball diamond, and any old hat or discarded box could become a base. It didn't take much, and we could go from zero to baseball in seconds!

We didn't need teams or an umpire and we never kept score; we were too busy having fun to care. Have you ever tried to catch a fly ball while you're laughing? It's not very effective, but it makes for a great time.

“It’s during those days when you’re just passing the time with the people you love . . . that prized memories are really made.”

As darkness fell and the fireflies came out, we knew the game was over. No expensive or thoroughly-planned activity could ever be sweeter than watching those kids chase fireflies on a warm Missouri summer night. I knew that even though we didn’t have money, we had everything worth having—family, love, and memories. I don’t have any pictures of those baseball games, but I can see them in my mind to this day.

materials

makes a 68"X 82" jellyroll quilt

QUILT TOP

- 1 jelly roll
- 2¾ yds background, sashing & inner border white
- ¾ yd cornerstones & second snowball corners yellow
- 1¼ yds outer border

BINDING

- ¾ yd coordinating fabric

BACKING

- 5 yds 44" wide **OR** 2¼ yds 90" wide

SAMPLE QUILT

- **Folklore** by Lily Ashbury for Moda
- **Bella Solids White** (98) by Moda
- **Bella Solids Yellow** (24) by Moda

1 sew

Select 3 jelly roll strips and sew lengthwise RST. Vary the lights and darks. Repeat.

Yield: 14 strip sets

2 cut

Subcut the strip sets into 6½" squares (6 per strip set). Make 80. Set aside. (4 leftover)

Yield: (80) 6½" x 6½" squares

From the white background fabric cut (20) 2½" strips. Subcut into 2½" squares (16 per strip).

Yield: (320) 2½" squares

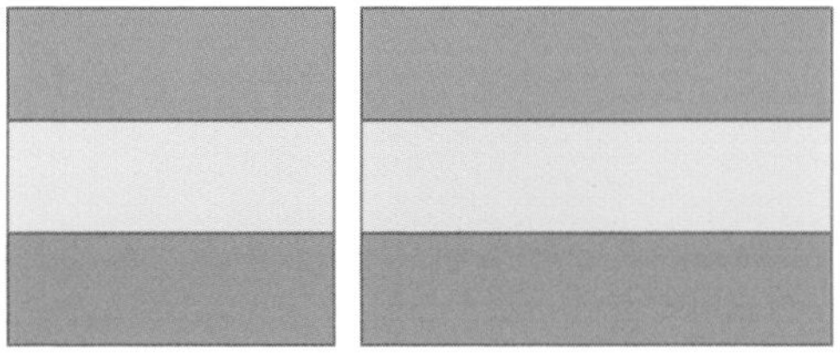

1 sew 3 strips together
2 subcut into 6½" squares

1 After the strips are sewn together, subcut into 6 ½" squares. Block size: 6½" x 6½"

2 Snowball each corner with a 2½" background solid square.

3 Snowball the corners again, but this time with 1½" yellow squares.

4 1½" sashing strips are added between blocks in a row. Horizontal sashing with cornerstones are added to the bottom of each row.

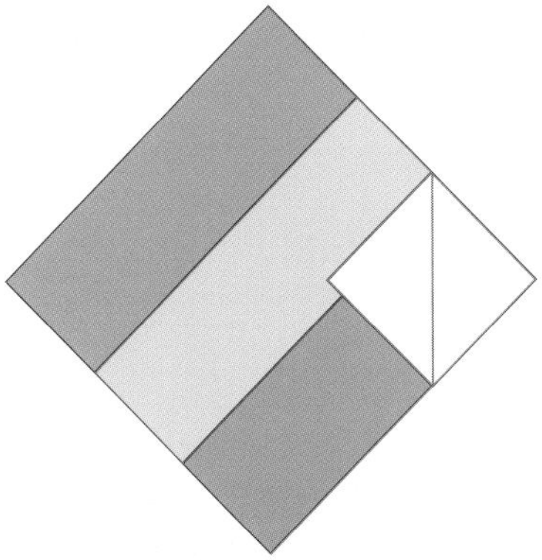

3 use the 2½" folded white squares to snowball the corner

TIP: *The folded line of the snowballing square should never point into the corner. Instead it should connect 2 sides of the block.*

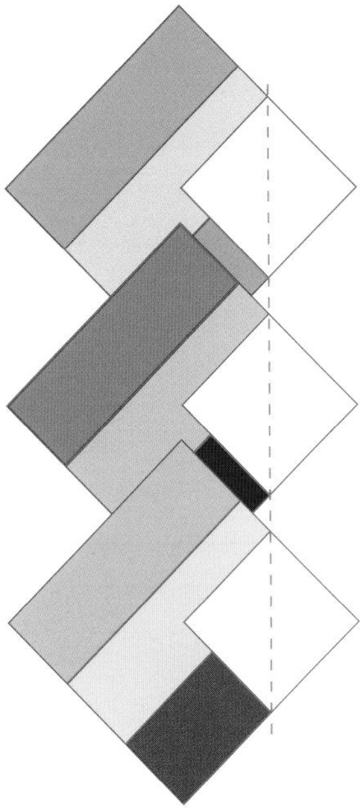

3A chain piecing one corner of all blocks in a row will speed up the process

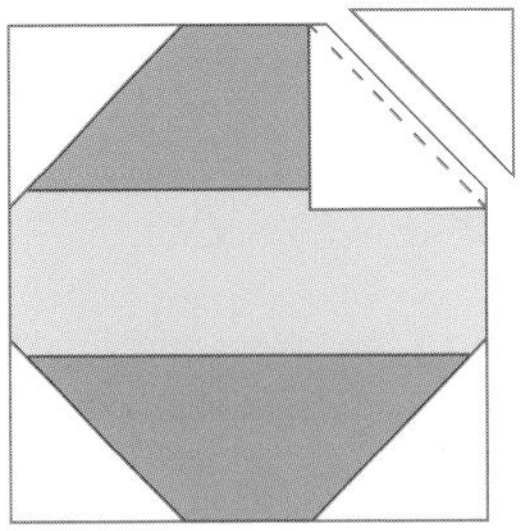

3B trim excess corner fabric ¼" from stitching; press to the corners

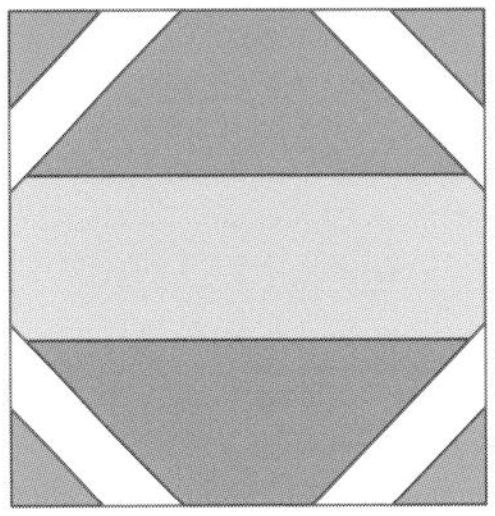

4 snowball the block again

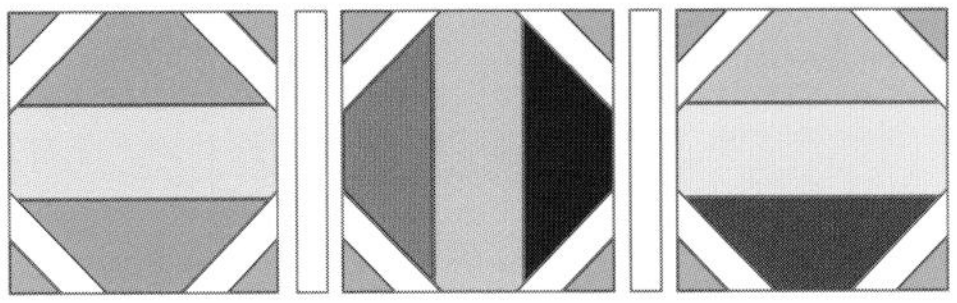

6 build rows with 8 blocks—every 2nd block turned ¼—and 7 sashing strips in between; alternate block orientation from row to row as well

3 snowball block

Snowballing a block gives the illusion of a rounded corner. Iron a diagonal line into the 2½" white squares. This is the sewing line. Lay the square on the block's corner and sew on the fold line. Chain piecing will speed things up. Feed a block with a 2½" square RST through the sewing machine. Continue sewing off the fabric a few stitches and feed the next block through the machine and so on. Snip threads to separate blocks. **3A** Trim excess fabric ¼" from the seam line. Press to the corner. Repeat for all 4 corners of each block. **3B**

Yield: 80 snowballed blocks

4 second snowball

Cut (14) 1½" strips of yellow fabric; subcut into 1½" squares. Set aside 63 squares for cornerstones. With the remaining 1½" squares, snowball the blocks again following the same process in step 3.

5 sashing

Cut (24) 1½" strips of white fabric; subcut into 1½" x 6½" rectangles—6 rectangles per strip. (2 are extra).

6 arrange & sew

In a 8 x 10 grid, lay out the blocks in an eye-pleasing fashion. Turn every other block ¼ so that the stripping runs horizontal, vertical, horizontal, vertical, etc. Carry this pattern from row to row as well. Begin sewing blocks into rows starting at the top left. Add a sashing strip between each block (7 per row between 8 blocks). Build 10 rows like this. Press to the sashing.

7 sew quilt center

Build the horizontal sashing using the remaining sashing strips and yellow 1½" squares. Sew 8 sashing strips together with 7 cornerstones between them to make a sashing row. **7A** Make 9. Press to the sashing.

7A make 9 horizontal sashing rows—8 sashing strips + 7 cornerstones

7B add horizontal sashing to the bottom of the first 9 rows; sew all rows together in sequence
8 attach inner & outer borders

Add 1 horizontal sashing row to the bottom of the first 9 rows. **7B** Then sew all 10 rows together in sequence. Press to sashing.

Quilt center size: 55½" x 69½"

8 borders

Cut (7) 1½" strips of inner border fabric. Find the average measurement of the quilt width (measure in three places). Cut 2 strips to that size, piecing strips together if necessary. Attach 1 to the top and 1 to the bottom. **A** & **B** Press to the borders.

Repeat for the sides measuring lengthwise. Include the newly attached borders in your measurements. Cut 2 strips to the average length, piecing strips together when needed. Attach 1 border to each side. **C** & **D** Press to the borders.

Cut (7) 5½" strips of outer border fabric. Attach to the quilt in the same manner as the inner border.

9 quilt & bind

Layer quilt top on batting and backing and quilt the way you like. Square up all raw edges.

Cut (8) 2½" strips from binding fabric. Piece together end-to-end with diagonal seams, aka *the plus sign method*.

Fold in half lengthwise, press. Attach to your quilt raw edges together with a ¼" seam.

Turn the folded binding edge to the back and tack in place with an invisible stitch or machine stitch if you like.

an American classic

quilt designed by HILLARY SPERRY

Independence Day is a big deal for the Doan family, full of memories and traditions, including quilts. Although there's nothing cozier than a quilt at Christmas time, the 4th of July just couldn't happen at our house without a few trusty, serviceable quilts.

We use our "car quilts," as we sometimes call them, because we leave them in the trunk of the car to be ready for use anytime we need them. Their first stop at the start of the day is the lawn, where they help us enjoy our annual picnic breakfast. I like to say a little maple syrup never hurt one of my quilts.

CAUTION

Before long those same quilts can be found saving spots on the curb where, shortly, a passel of grandchildren gather to sit in the shade and watch the 4th of July Parade. Once the last dance troupe and fire engine have headed for home, we stretch our legs, fold up our quilts, and head back to my place.

In the evening, the kids run around the lawn swirling sparklers through the summer air, and when it starts to get dark, we cluster together on quilts spread on the grass. I snag whichever grandkids are closest and most willing to snuggle, then my brothers bring out their fireworks stash and put on a show for us. As the last sparks fizzle out, we get quiet, and that's when Ron reads the names of all our family members that have served our country in the armed forces.

Like most Americans, I come from a family of immigrants, and though I treasure my Swedish roots, I was taught to be always grateful for the great blessing of living in America. I feel such a deep love for my country, the Land of Promise, and the many opportunities and freedoms I enjoy. After a long, fun-filled 4th, it feels so special to be able to sit on a quilt under the stars with my loved ones and think about how blessed we really are.

THE DOAN FAMILY HAS ALWAYS ENJOYED small town parades. Here we are celebrating the 200th birthday of the US Constitution.

A FUN TRICK
NOISE MAKER
HANDLE CAREFULLY

materials

makes a 55" X 64" charm pack quilt

QUILT TOP

- 1 charm pack blue
- 1 charm pack white
- 1¼ yd blue
- 1¼ yd white

BINDING

- ½ yd coordinating fabric

BACKING

- 3½ yds 44" wide OR 1¾ yds 90" wide

SAMPLE QUILT

- **Bella Solids White** (98) by Moda
- **Bella Solids Admiral Blue** (48) by Moda

1 cut & sew

Cut (16) 2¼" strips of blue fabric.
Cut (16) 2¼" strips of white fabric.

Sew 1 blue and 1 white strip RST lengthwise.

Yield: (16) blue/white strip pairs.

Layer 2 strip sets RST matching opposite colors, i.e. white to blue; blue to white. 1A Sew the strips together on both raw edges with a ¼" seam, making a tube. Repeat with remaining strip sets. 1B

Yield: (8) blue/white tubes

TIP: *Watch out! These are 2¼" strips—not 2½"!*

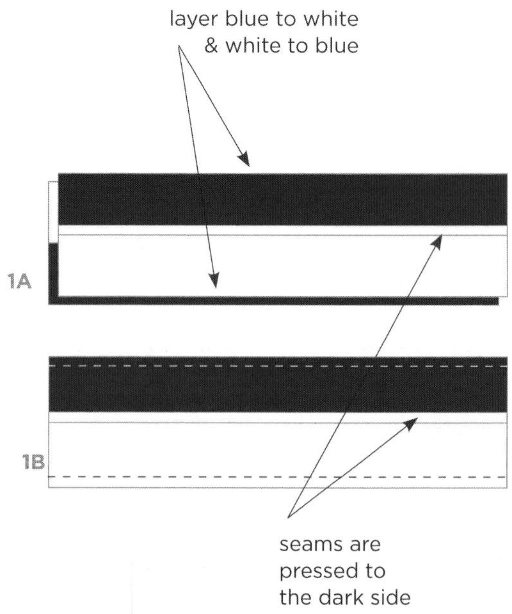

2 cut

Use any ruler 5″ or larger that has a 45° line marked. Place the 45° line on the stitched seam at the top. If you are right-handed start at the far right side; left-handed, at the far left.

Make the first cut and toss the scrap. 2A Now slide the ruler down to the bottom line of stitching, aligning the 45° ruler line to it. Follow the direction of the arrow, moving the ruler along the edge of the fabric that was just cut.

Make your second cut when the tip of the ruler meets the seam and the 45° line aligns with the stitching. 2B
1 block cut.

Again following the direction of the arrow, move the ruler back up to the top line of stitching along the newly cut edge. Continue in this fashion with all the strip tubes.

Yield: 11 blocks per strip;
84 striped blocks needed

3 arrange & sew

After you've pressed all the striped blocks open (seams to the dark side), you're ready to lay out the quilt in a 12 x 14 grid. This is where the magic happens. The quilt consists of only 2 rows (blue & white) that alternate striped squares with charm squares.

Blue row: Begin with a blue charm square, followed by a striped block with its blue corner facing up to the right. Continue across. 3A

White Row: Begin with a striped block, white corner facing up to the right. Follow with a white charm square and so on. 3B

Repeat these 2 rows 7 times, 14 rows total.

Start at the top left and sew blocks together side to side across in rows. Press all seams to the charms squares. This will facilitate nesting when rows are sewn together.

Sew rows together top to bottom nesting seams as you go.

Quilt center: 54½″ x 63½″

4 quilt & bind

Layer quilt top on batting and backing and quilt the way you like. Square up all raw edges.

Cut (6) 2½″ strips from binding fabric. Piece together end-to-end with diagonal seams, aka *the plus sign method.*

Fold in half lengthwise, press. Attach to your quilt raw edges together with a ¼″ seam.

Turn the folded binding edge to the back and tack in place with an invisible stitch or machine stitch if you like.

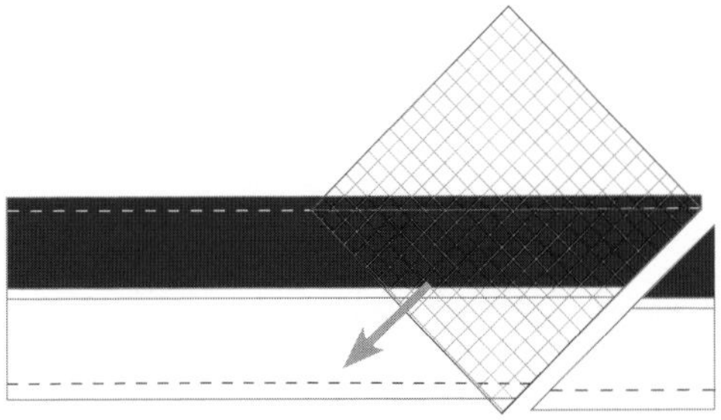

2A the far right corner of the ruler is positioned on the stitching; cut, then slide down

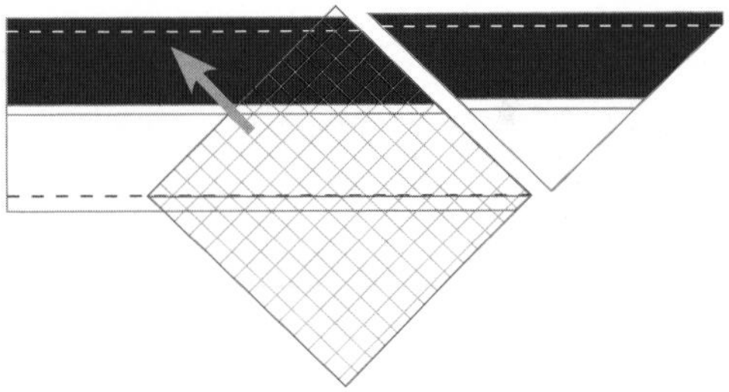

2B again, the far right corner of the ruler is positioned on the stitching; cut, then slide up

3A *blue row:* solid charm + striped block with blue corner upper right: 12 across

3B *white row:* striped block with white corner upper right + white charm square: 12 across

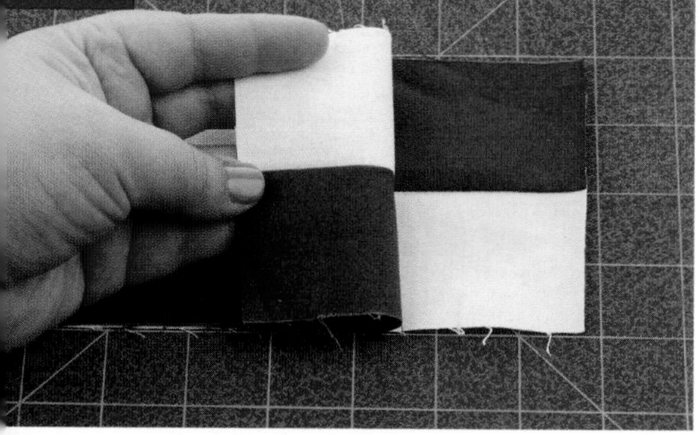

1 Layer 2 strip sets matching opposite colors.

2 Align the 45 degree line of the ruler onto the line of stitching. Cut through all layers of the strip tube.

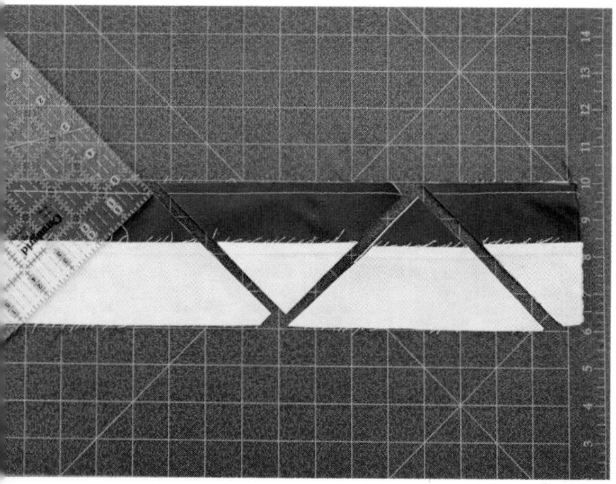

3 You will be cutting in zig-zag fashion.

YOU WILL BE AMAZED at how quickly this classic pattern comes together! Our simple pattern, combined with precut fabric makes this quilt a snap!

it's in the Bag

bag designed by STEPHEN NIXDORF

When I was pregnant with my second baby, my mother-in-law gifted me the hugest diaper bag in all creation. It was cute and very stylish, but just seemed so unnecessarily gigantic. As I snipped off the tags, I noticed the warning "Not For Use As Infant Carrier." I chuckled to myself, thinking that this bag was large enough to carry not just my baby, but the two-year-old as well. Heck, I could probably toss in a few of the neighbor kids, the dog, and even have room for the kitchen sink, just in case! I appreciated the gift, but assumed I would never need to actually make full use of the massive bag.

Three weeks later, I was home from the hospital with my new little bundle of joy. I pulled out the gargantuan diaper bag and began to pack it for our first outing to Grandma's house. A handful of diapers for the toddler. Two handfuls of diapers for the baby. A package of wipes. A burp cloth. A second burp cloth, just in case.

"The bag wasn't even close to full, and I began to wonder if it had been manufactured in the same factory as Mary Poppins' famously bottomless carpet bag."

An extra outfit for baby. A jacket for the toddler. Pajamas for both. The bag wasn't even close to full, and I began to wonder if it had been manufactured in the same factory as Mary Poppins' famously bottomless carpet bag.

Time raced by as it so often does, and in just a few short years, along came baby number three. Packing the bag for simple outings became even more ridiculous: extra pants for the four-year-old in case of an accident. Diapers, diapers, DIAPERS. A bib for my incredibly messy two year old. Diaper rash cream. A handful of matchbox cars (because we never went ANYWHERE without matchbox cars!). A camera to capture every cute moment. Band aids. Hand sanitizer. A back-up pacifier for the two year-old (heaven forbid we find ourselves without a pacifier!). Sunscreen and a hat for each of my super-burnable kiddos. A stack of library books that needed to be dropped off on the way. And lastly, an assortment of emergency snacks. At last the bag was filled to capacity. But somehow, in an act that seemed to defy known physics, it still managed to zip shut!

I guess I never really got over the habit of packing any and every needful thing with me wherever I go. That's why I love projects like this Tumbler Bag. As practical as it is cute, this is a bag that will get tons of use. It could even be used as a stylish diaper bag. Just be sure to never use it to carry around the baby!

materials

makes a charm pack tumbler bag

BAG

- 1 charm pack
- ¾ contrasting fabric for: bag band, strap, loop & pockets
- ½ yd lining

INTERFACING

- 2 yds Pellon shape flex 101 fusible woven interfacing

TOOLS

- MSQC 5″ tumbler template

SAMPLE BAG

- **Hot Collective** by Kaffe Fassett for Rowan/Westminster Fibers

1 select & cut

Use the *MSQC 5″ Tumbler Template* to cut 40 tumblers from the charm pack squares. Each side of the outer bag consists of 20 tumblers.

2 create panels

Fabric for the outer bag's panels is created by piecing tumblers together in 4 rows of 5. Arrange 20 tumblers in an eye-pleasing grid. 2A Make 2.

Sew tumblers together side-to-side first. Offset the tumblers at the ¼″ seam allowance. 2B This creates "dog ears" and will ensure the tumblers line up in a straight line once they have been sewn and pressed.

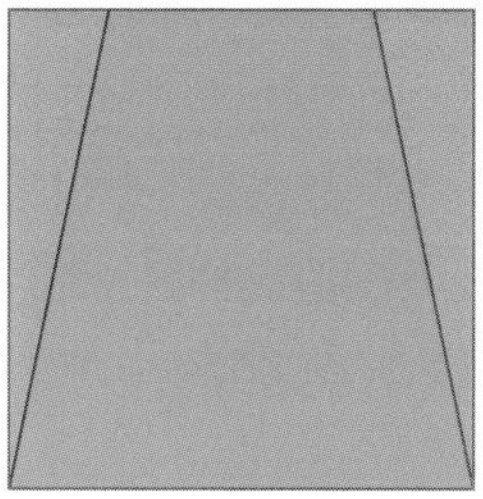

1 cut 40 tumbler shapes from charm squares

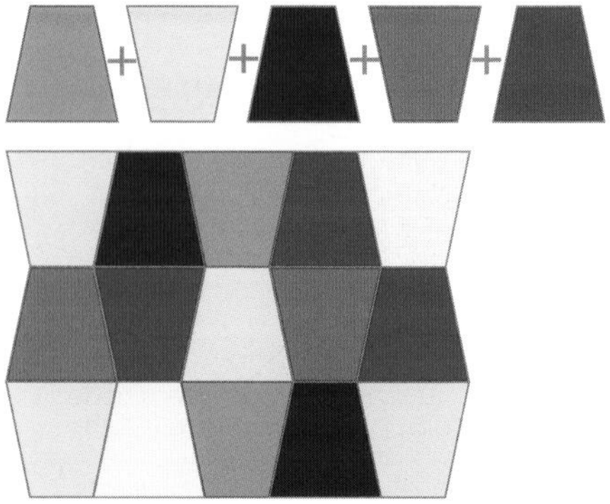

2A arrange 20 tumblers into 4 rows of 5

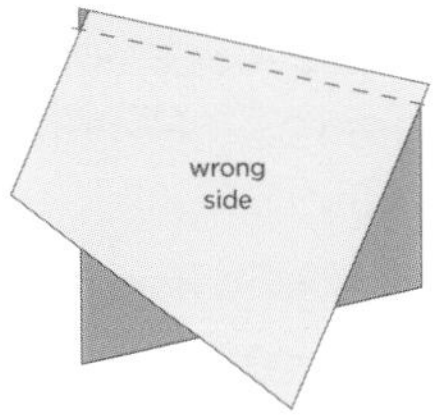

2B Create dog ears by offsetting the tumblers at the ¼″ seam allowance

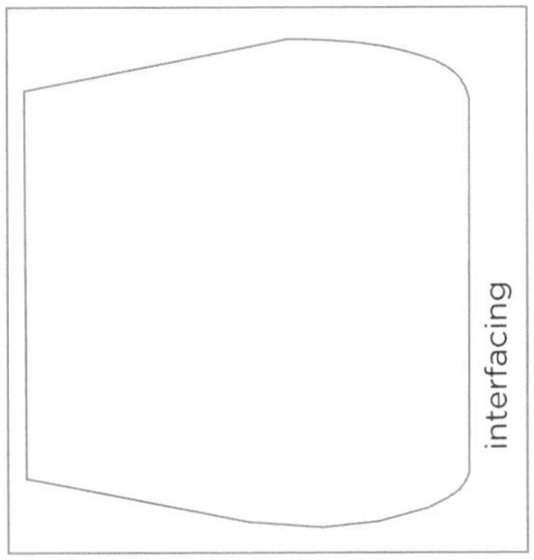

4 cut out interfacing for outer bag

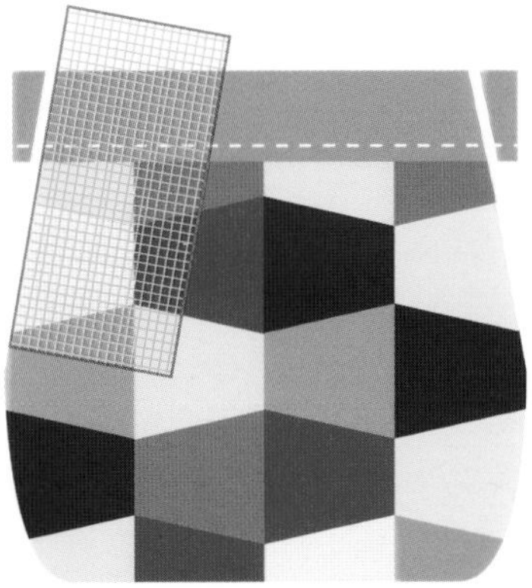

5 attach a band to the top of each outer bag panel; extend the angle

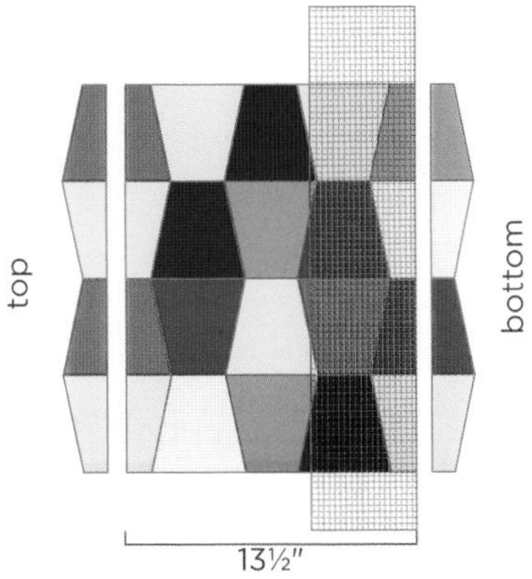

3A cut tumblers along a zig-zag edge in half; measure from this edge 13½″ and straighten the 2nd zig-zag edge

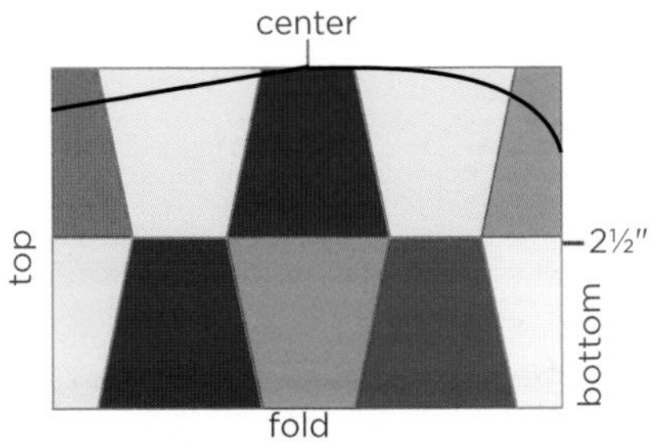

3B fold the fabric in half; lay the pattern's dotted line on the fold; the curve is cut on the opposite side

Press all seams in the even rows to the right; in the odd rows to the left. This will make nesting seams easier.

Sew rows together nesting seams as you go to complete the "fabric."

3 trim & shape

Using a ruler and rotary cutter, trim the 4 tumblers of one zig-zag edge straight by cutting them in half. Measure 13½″ from this side and trim the other zig-zag edge. Don't worry about the cut being exactly in the middle of that row. These edges are the top & bottom of the bag. 3A

Make 2 entire panels.

Fold the fabric of one panel in half. *The bag pattern insert:* cut along the solid curved edge of the pattern. Fold along the solid straight line between the outer bag and the bag lining. Align the dotted line to the fold, matching the top & bottom to both trimmed edges. Cut along the curve. Make 2 outer bag panels. 3B

Yield: 2 shaped outer bag panels

4 interfacing

Use the outer bag pattern to cut out interfacing for each panel. Keep the pattern folded at the solid straight line for the correct height. Adhere the interfacing to the wrong side of each panel. Make sure the bumpy texture is against the fabric. Press using steam on both sides.

5 contrasting band

From the contrasting fabric cut a 3½″ strip. Cut (2) 18″ rectangles from the strip and apply interfacing to both on the wrong side. Use the pattern to make 2 bands. Trace the band pattern onto tissue paper. Fold an 18″ rectangle in half and match the dotted line of the pattern to the fold. Cut. Make 2.

Sew 1 band to the top of each outer bag panel with ½″ seam allowance. Press to the band and top stitch ⅛″ next to the seam line. If you wish, use the triple stitch wherever top stitching is needed.

If necessary, trim the band to the same angle as the outer bag panel.

6A sew outer bag panels together;

6 sew outer panels

With fabric panels RST align the band seams and sew the sides and bottom closed. Use ½″ seam allowance back-stitching at both ends. **6A**

To form gussets, open the seams flat and match the side to the bottom seam at the corner forming a V shape. From the corner's tip, mark 1″ down the center and 2½″ on the folded sides. **6B** Use a pencil to connect those points. Sew along this line backstitching at the beginning and end. Trim to a ¼.″ Turn right side out. Gently push out corners. Set aside.

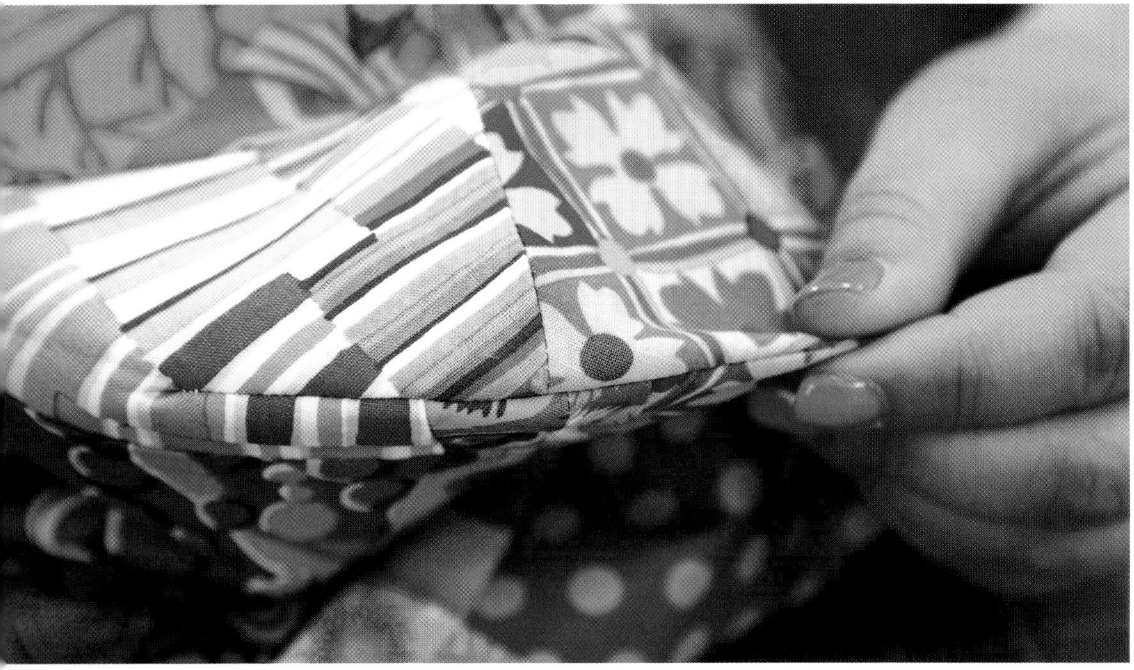

A look at the finished gusset.

7 lining

From the ½ yd lining fabric cut away the selvages. Measure 15½″ from this edge and cut off the fold. Set this piece aside for pockets if you wish. Use the bag lining pattern to cut 2 lining pieces from the 15½″ x 18″ fabric. Set the bottom of the pattern on the 18″ side. If the lining is a tad shorter than the bag lining pattern, it will not be a problem. Cut out the lining. Cut out the interfacing and fuse to the back of the lining. If you wish to make 2 interior pockets for your bag go to **msqc.co/tumbler** on the web for those additional instructions. Otherwise follow step 6 above and sew the lining together. Make the gussets but do NOT turn right side out yet.

8 strap & button loop

From the contrasting fabric, cut a 5″ strip WOF. Iron the strip in half lengthwise; open; then fold both sides to the center fold. Press. Close the first fold. There are now four layers. **8A** Top stitch lengthwise along both edges, using the triple stitch if you wish. **8B**

Create a button loop in the same manner but from a 4″ x 12″ rectangle. Find the center and flip both ends up 90° from that point, creating a "V." Press. Overlap the ends ⅛″ and tack into place. Tack the triangle into place as well. Tack the loop again to the size of the button, creating a buttonhole. **8C**

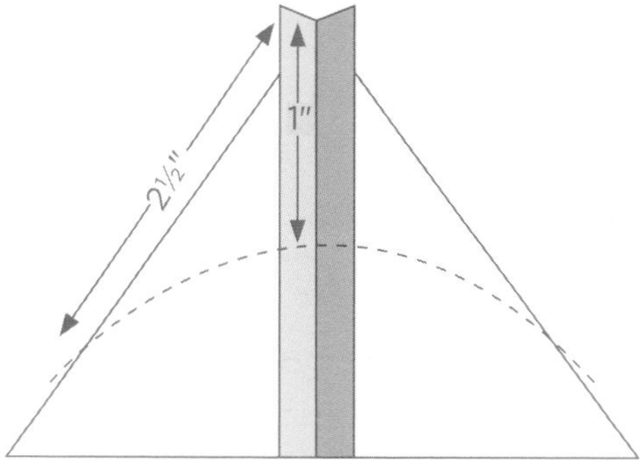

6B make the gusset; trim to ¼"

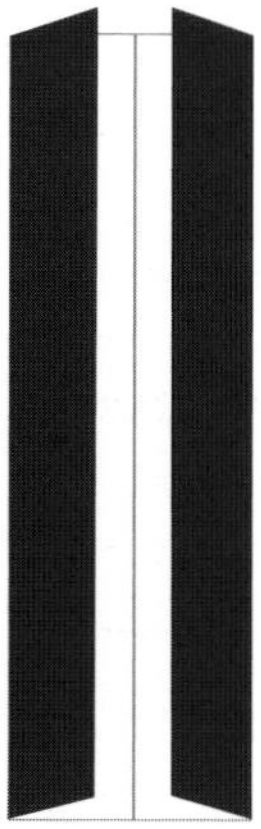

8A fold both sides to the center; fold closed

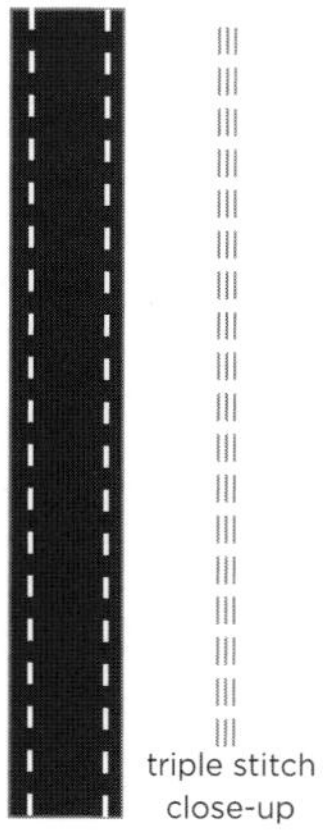

8B topstitch

8C create a "V" at the center of the buttonhole loop strip; tack into place (right side view)

9 finishing

Place the raw ends of the handle along the top edge of the outer panel at the side seams. Careful not to twist it. Pin into place. Center the button loop on the back-side of the bag RST. Pin. If you want, baste straps & loop into place.

Slide the completed outer bag inside the lining that is still wrong side out. They will be RST. Make sure the strap and button loop are down between the two layers. Match raw edges along the top opening, lining up the side seams. Pin together. Sew ½" seam all around the top leaving a 6" opening. Back-stitch at the beginning and end.

Pull bag through the opening. Stuff the inner lining back into the outer bag. Gently push the gussets into shape. At the top, roll the lining slightly to the inside and iron into place. Tuck the seam allowances of the opening to the inside and press. Top stitch ⅛" around the entire top edge of the bag to close the opening and give a finished look.

Add a button to the front band.

Bloom & Grow

wall hanging designed by JENNY DOAN

I'm a sucker for flowers, but I must admit I'm picky. You, see flowers that are cut for a bouquet or centerpiece are lovely for only a few short days before they start to wither and droop. After they're tossed into the trash, I'm left with nothing more than an empty vase. What a waste! No, I prefer flowers with roots. I've always said that I would much rather receive a flat of pansies to plant in the garden than a big, expensive bouquet of roses. (Not that I don't love roses, but my husband knows that if he's going to give me roses, they better be on a bush!) It's just such a joy to watch things grow, take root, and thrive while becoming increasingly more beautiful over time.

Years ago when we moved into our first home, I was pregnant with our first child and we were anxious to prepare a cozy nest to house our new little family. Our new place wasn't large or fancy, but it fit our budget

perfectly. The house had been neglected by a long string of careless owners, so we spent many hours that winter scrubbing, patching, and painting the interior to make it feel like home. As I worked, I tried to imagine myself as a new mother in those very rooms. I often worried that I wouldn't know how to care for a such a tiny, helpless little human. How could I be in charge of an entire life? As winter turned to spring, my fears grew as steadily as my ever-expanding belly.

When the snow finally began to melt, I decided to venture out for the first time to really explore the overgrown yard of our new home. As I wandered, I discovered fruit trees, massive lilac bushes, and a dozen or so rose bushes. There were strawberry plants, day lilies, tulips, and hyacinths just starting to peek out of the newly-thawed soil. It made me happy to think that, at some point in the past, someone had cared for this house. Someone had planted these trees and flowers with a sense of hope for the future—a future filled with freshly picked cherries, nectarines, and strawberries, and made more beautiful by a rainbow of flowers.

You see, these plants had long ago taken root. I'll never know how many years that yard had been left untended, but to this day I am amazed that after such extended neglect these plants were able to continue to grow and thrive on their own. Certainly it was the roots, strong and resilient, that made it possible for the plants to survive.

“Just like the roots in my backyard garden, these memories gave me the strength I needed to grow into my new role of motherhood.”

Time passed (as it always does), and before I knew it, I was mother to the most perfect little baby in the world. Day by day my fears of the difficulties of motherhood were replaced with happy confidence. I found myself relying on the example of my own mother in even the simplest of situations. Within my mind and my heart, I held a hundred moments of her love and wisdom that I hadn't even realized had been tucked away in my memory. Just like the roots in my backyard garden, these memories gave me the strength I needed to grow into my new role of motherhood.

Each of us has our own “roots”—family, faith, life experiences, etc. These roots keep us grounded and inspire us to do great things. Like the resilient plants in my backyard, if we grow our roots deep enough, we will be able to weather whatever comes and eventually blossom into the very thing we're meant to become.

HAND APPLIQUÉ DOESN'T HAVE TO BE COMPLICATED OR SCARY. It's really just a hidden stitch that keeps your work secure until the machine quilting stitches it firmly in place!

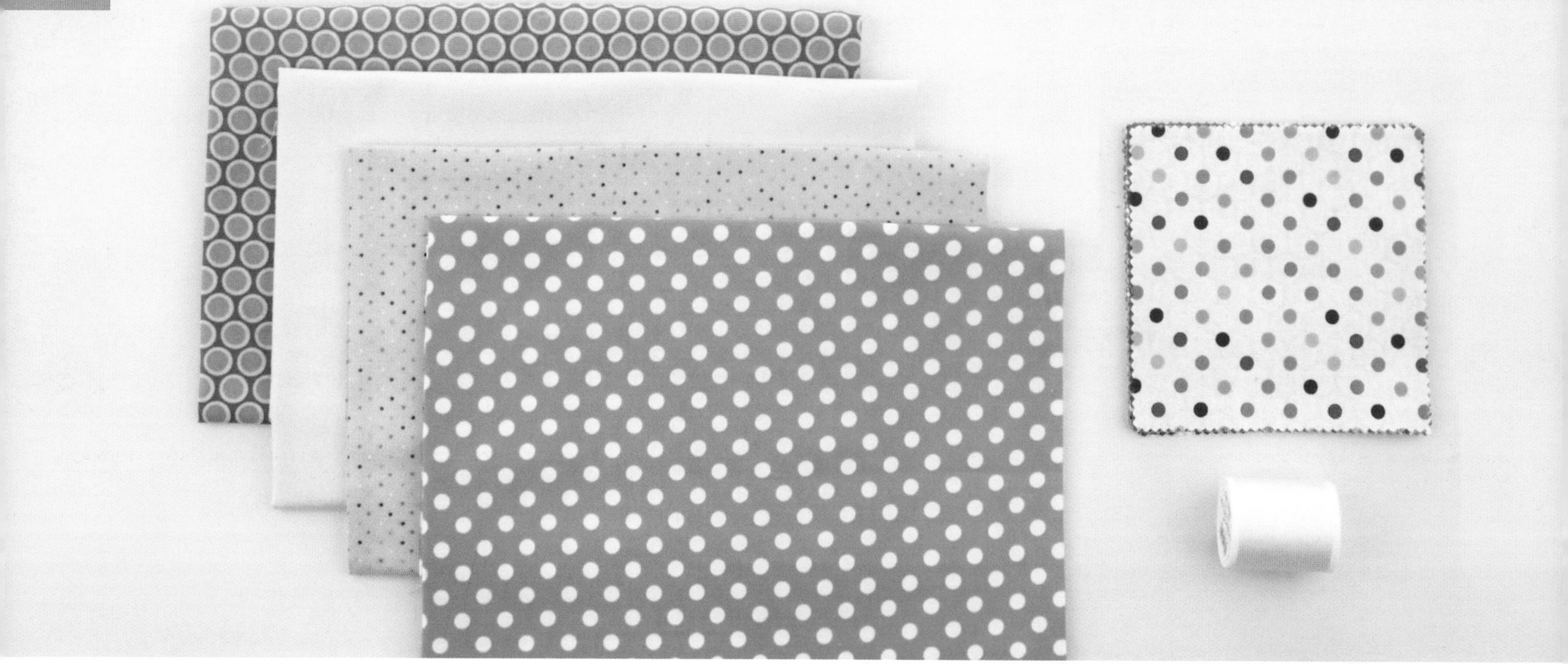

materials

makes a 28½" X 38½" wall hanging

QUILT TOP
- 1 charm pack prints
- (1) 2½" strip for stems & leaves
- (2) 10" layer cakes for pot
- ¾ yd background

BINDING
- ½ yd coordinating fabric

BACKING
- 1 yd coordinating fabric

ADDITIONAL TOOLS
- 10" Tumbler shape
- Layer Cake Dresden Plate Ruler

SAMPLE QUILT
- **Windham Basic Brights** by Windham

1 cut

From the background yardage cut a 24" x 36" rectangle.

All the "petals" for the flowers are cut using the *Dresden Ruler*. Keep the petals for each flower together.

Small Flower (18 petals): Select 3 charm squares. Cut them in half.
Yield: (6) 2½" x 5" rectangles.

Use the 2½" mark on the ruler to cut each rectangle into 3 blades. Flip the ruler each cut. Set aside. 1A

Medium Flower (20 petals): From 10 charm squares, cut 2 petals per square using the 5" mark on the ruler. Flip the ruler for the second petal. Set aside. 1B

Large Flower (10 petals): Select 10 charm squares. Iron a crease down the middle of each square. Align the ruler's center to the fold. Set the wide top of the ruler on one side. With a fabric marking tool, mark the width of the ruler. Slide the ruler up, setting the ruler's narrow edge on the opposite side. Mark the width of the ruler's narrow tip, keeping it centered on the fold. Connect the marks on each side and cut along those lines. 1C-E

Of the remaining charm squares set 2 aside & cut 17 in half. These half-charms are for the pieced border and picket fence.

Yield: (34) 2½" x 5" rectangles

1 After sewing across the widest side, clip the folded corner to reduce bulk.

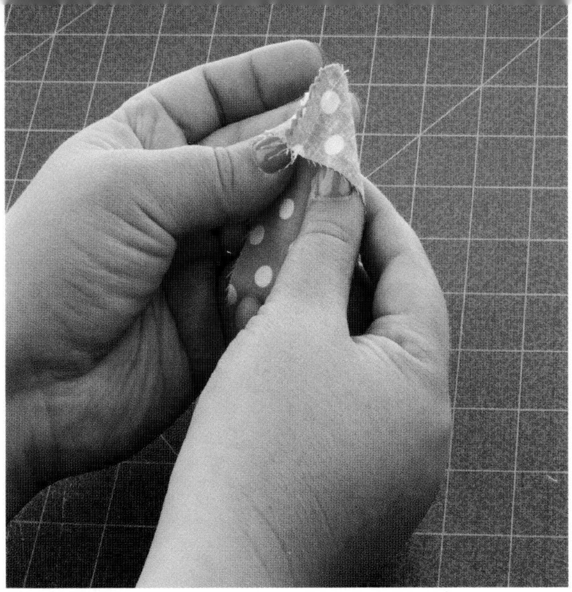

2 Turn the V right side out and gently push out the tip.

3 The seam ends up in the back. The front has a nicely finished shape.

4 Sew all the petals together. Press all seams to the same side.

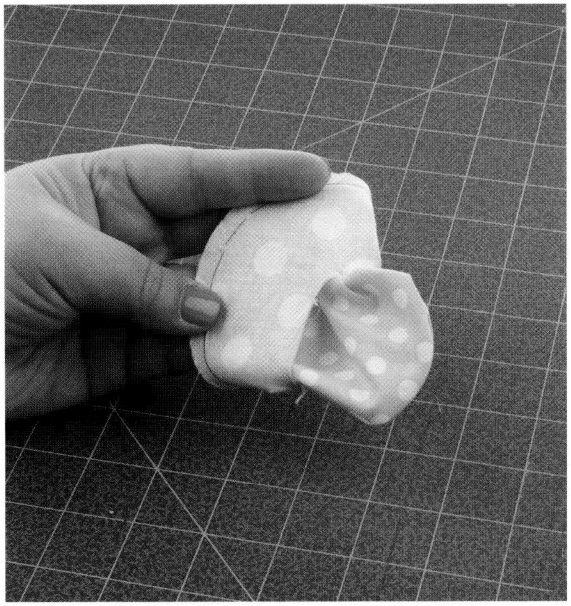

5 Lining technique: sew the shape closed around the layer edge. Slit one side open and turn right side out.

6 Lines have been drawn to show placement of the flower pot and stems. Make sure the leaves are tucked in far enough so that the stitching will capture their raw edges.

2 sew the points

Chain piecing will speed this step up. Fold blade in half lengthwise RST. Sew across the top at the widest end. Clip the seam allowance 45° at the folded edge to reduce bulk. Turn the corner right side out, pushing the seam allowance to one side. Flip to the back. Center the seam down the middle creating a point. Press. Repeat for all flower petals and for 12 half charm rectangles.

3 fence & flowers

Begin with the picket fence. Sew 12 "pickets" together side-by-side in a row using a ¼" seam. Press seams to one side in the same direction, strengthening the seam.

Do the same for each flower's petals except that these will naturally form a circle. Make 3 flowers. Pin the flowers into position on the background.

Position the picket fence along the bottom 24" side of the background, raw edges together. Baste the fence to the background along this edge at ⅛." Pin the picket points.

4 pot & centers

Use the 10" *Tumbler Ruler* to cut 2 pots from the 2 layer cakes. RST sew the pots together around the entire shape. Clip the corners. Slice open the "lining" pot and turn inside out pushing out the

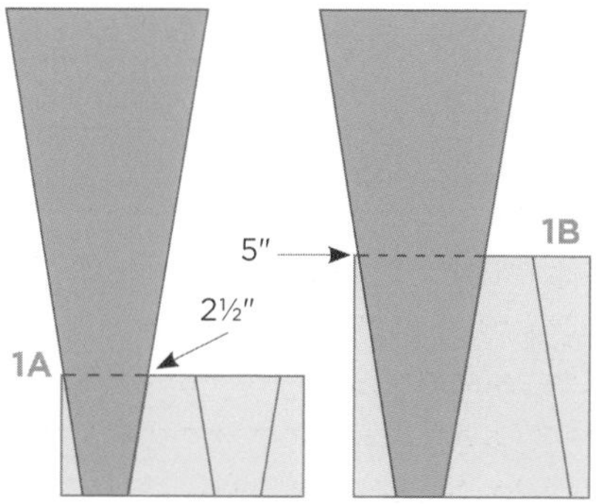

1A small flower: cut (3) 2½" dresden shapes from (6) ½ charm squares

1B medium flower: cut (2) 5" dresden shapes from 10 charm squares

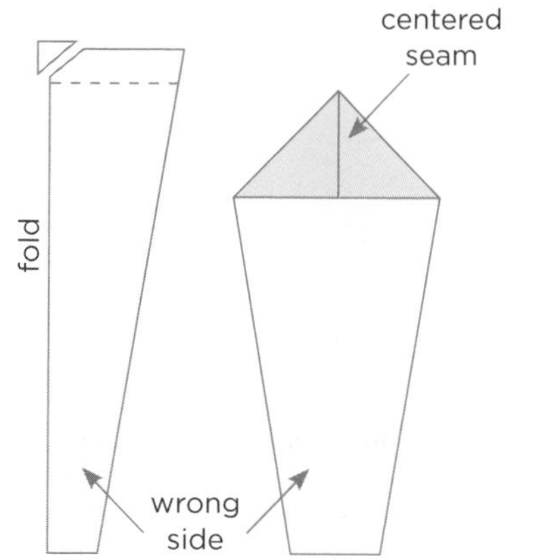

2 fold petals & pickets in half RST; sew across wide end; clip folded corner; turn & press

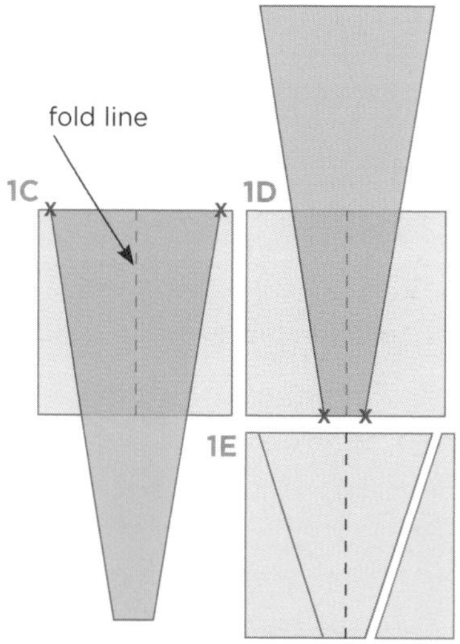

1C-E large flower: mark (**X**) the wide and narrow end of a dresden shape on the top & bottom of a 5" charm square; keep the ruler centered on the fold line; cut that shape.

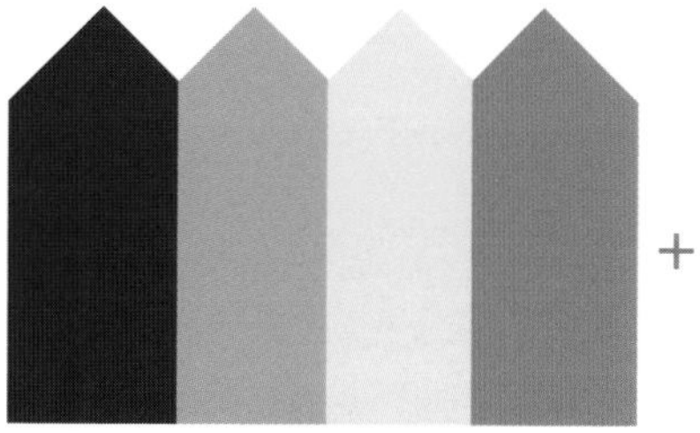

3 assemble picket fence

3 assemble flower petals

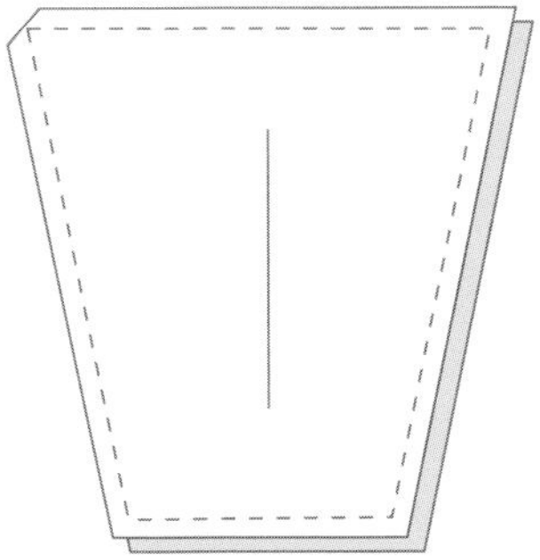

4 *lining technique:* RST sew ¼″ all around; clip corners; slit one layer; turn inside out; press into shape

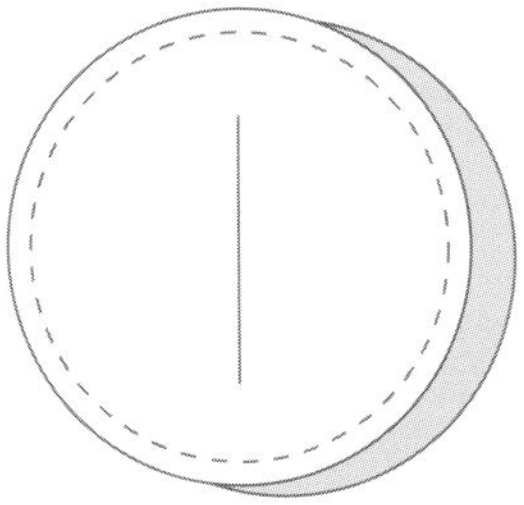

4 use the *lining technique* for flower centers; suggested cut sizes: 6¾″, 5″ & 4½″

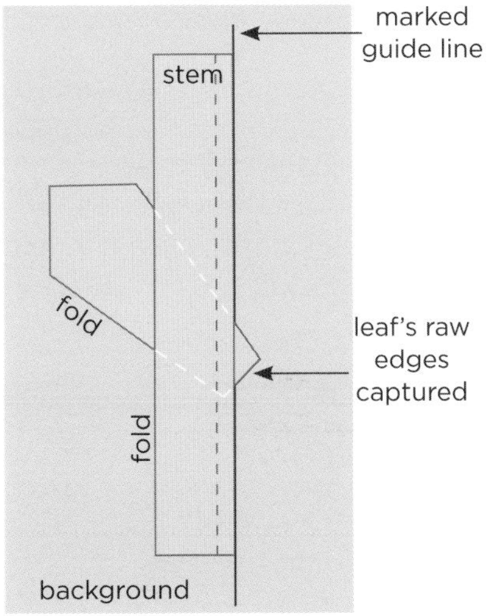

5 position the leaf far enough to the right that the stem's seam will capture them

corners gently. Press. Pin right side up into place above the picket fence.

Use this same "lining" technique to make the flower centers. From the binding fabric cut (4) 2½″ strips. Set aside. Cut 3 pairs of circles for centers using any round glass, plate or ruler that will give you the size center you want. Clip the curves. Pin into place. (As an alternative, use the 2 remaining charms for the smaller flower centers; cut their linings from the binding fabric.)

5 stems & leaves

Iron the 2½″ green strip in half lengthwise. Determine the position and length of each stem. Use a pencil to trace along the raw edge of the stem. This will be a sewing guide line. Include an extra ½″ so that the raw ends will tuck ¼″ beneath the flower and the pot. Cut 3 stems.

From the 2½″ green strip make 3 leaves as in steps 1 & 2 for the small flower using the 2½″ size. After making the point, press the side edges under ¼." Place the leaf's raw end beyond the marked line. This way they will be captured by the stem's seam. Pin in place.

With the long raw edge of the stem placed along the marked line, sew a ¼″ seam, fully capturing the ends of the leaves as you go. Make sure the short ends are covered by a flower and the pot. Fold the stem strip over the raw edge encasing it.

6 finishing

Appliqué all the elements into place by hand or machine: stems first, then leaves, picket points, flower petals, flower centers and flower pot. A blanket, straight or zig-zag stitch is recommended for machine appliqué.

From the remaining rectangles, sew 2 strips of 8 rectangles end-to-end and attach to either side. Trim any excess. For the top sew 6 rectangles together, attach and trim. Layer with batting and backing, quilt. Trim and bind using the (4) 2½″ strips that were set aside.

My favorite kind of movie stars

quilt designed by JENNY DOAN

When the kids were teenagers we loved to have outdoor movie nights. It was nothing elaborate, no fancy projector or big screen. Nope, we'd just spread our quilts on the lawn and set the television out on the front porch. It may sound kind of odd, but we had heaps of fun laying out under the stars with a big bowl of popcorn and a good movie playing. The kids often invited their friends over and we all had a great time.

Providing simple, wholesome activities like this for my family brought me joy. It didn't take a lot

> "A charm quilt feels more cozy, more relaxed. It just feels right to take it along wherever you go: to the park, to the ball-game, or on a campout."

of planning or money, but over the years I've learned that these uncomplicated, inexpensive family traditions often become the most cherished memories. Simplicity can be a beautiful thing.

I have always loved simple charm quilts. It seems that whenever I make a quilt that is just basic squares, it is one of the first to sell out of my shop. I think it's the simplicity that appeals to folks. These are quilts that you can really cozy up in.

I consider myself a practical quilter. If you've spent hour upon hour painstakingly piecing an elaborate double wedding ring quilt, you may not want to spread it out on the ground for a picnic or drag it to the beach. It feels too special, too precious for everyday casual use. But a charm quilt feels more cozy, more relaxed. It just feels right to take it along wherever you go: to the park, to the ballgame, or on a campout. You don't fear sticky fingers or wet grass. A quilt like this can be tossed in the car, washed a hundred times, patched and re-patched, and used and loved to the very last thread.

Every now and again it's fun to treat yourself to something really elegant, like high tea at a fancy hotel, box seats at the opera, or even cooking with obscenely expensive pink salt from the Himalayas! But I find that, most of the time, I'm quite happy with the simple, uncomplicated joys of everyday life. Give me my family, a comfy quilt, and a TV on the front porch, and I'm one happy gal!

***THIS QUILT IS A GREAT WAY TO ACCENTUATE A SINGLE BLOCK.** We all have orphan blocks leftover from quilt projects. Use them up in a similar manner by surrounding them with charm squares, or even large pieces of fabric. Who knows what you can come up with!*

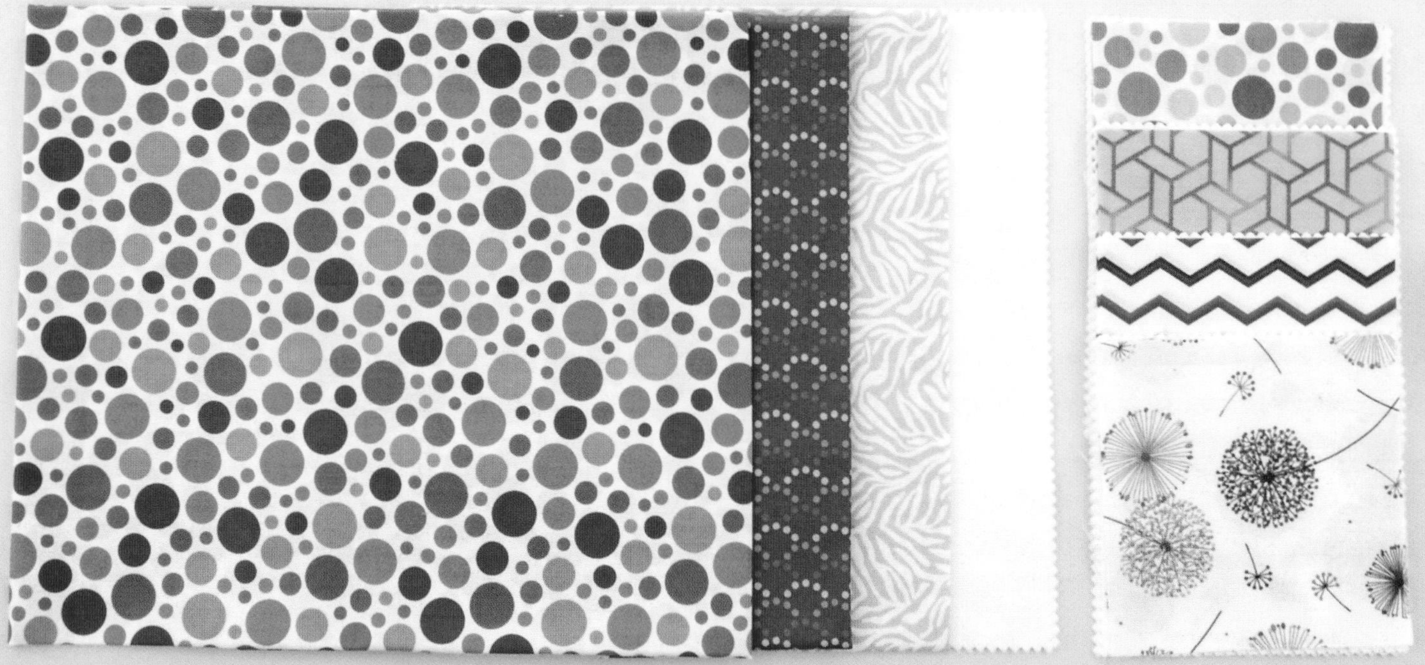

materials

makes a 65"x 83" charm quilt

QUILT TOP

- 4 charm packs
- 2 fat quarters for star
- 1 yd inner border & background
- ¾ yd outer border

BINDING

- ¾ yd coordinating fabric

BACKING

- 5 yds 44" wide **OR** 2 yds 90" wide

SAMPLE QUILT

- **Soho** by Studio 8 for Quilting Treasures
- **Bella Solids Bleached White** (98) by Moda

1 large star

From 2 star fat quarters cut:
(4) 10" squares
From background yardage cut:
(2) 10" squares from (1) 10" strip
(4) 6⅛" squares from (1) 6⅛" strip

Layer 2 star 10" squares RST. Sew ¼" around the outside perimeter. 1A Cut diagonally twice. For this step try a small mat that can be picked up and turned, or a rotating cutting mat. 1B Press open.

Yield: (4) star HSTs (star center)

With the remaining (4) 10" squares, make (2) pairs of 1 print & 1 solid each. Use the same method as before to make HSTs.

Yield: (8) print/solid HSTs (star legs)

1A pair the 2 layer cakes RST; sew ¼" around the outside

1B cut both diagonals; 4 HSTs per layer cake pair

1 Pair 2 layer cakes and sew ¼″ around all edges. Then cut through both diagonally.

2 Make a second diagonal cut. Try not to move the fabric. Instead use a small cutting mat that can be picked up and turned—or use a rotating cutting mat.

3 There are now 4 HSTs (half square triangles).

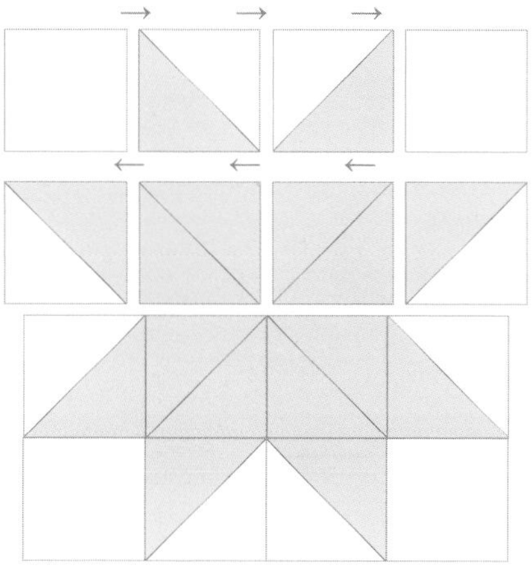

1C build the star as shown; press seams in opposite directions from row to row

Square up all HSTs to 6⅛.″ Layout the star elements on a table. 1C Sew the blocks together to build rows; follow pressing arrows; then sew rows together to complete the block.

Star block: 23″ x 23″

2 quilt center

The quilt is layed out in a 12 x 16 grid pattern—except that the large star will replace a 5 x 5 section of 5″ charm squares. Use all but 1 charm square from the packs. Lay the squares out in the following manner, looking for an even balance of lights and darks:

A: 2 rows of 12
B: 5 rows of 2; large star; 5 rows of 5
C: 9 rows of 12

Section A: Begin at the top left sewing blocks together across, then sewing the 2 rows together. Press even rows in one direction; odd rows in the opposite direction. Nest seams as you go. Set aside.

Section B: Build the 5 rows of 2 charm squares; then the 5 rows of 5. Sandwich the large star between these two sections. Set aside.

Section C: Sew rows of 12 blocks together 9 times. Complete the section by sewing all rows to each other.

Finish the quilt center by sewing each section to the next in sequence.

Quilt center size: 54½″ x 72½″

3 borders

Cut (7) 2½" strips of inner border fabric. Find the average measurement of the quilt width (measure in three places). Cut 2 strips to that size and attach to the top and bottom. A & B Press to the borders.

Repeat for the sides measuring lengthwise. Include the newly attached borders in your measurements. Cut 2 strips to the average length. Piece strips together when needed. Attach 1 border to each side. C & D Press to the borders.

Cut (7) 3½" strips of outer border fabric. Attach to the quilt in the same manner as the inner border.

4 quilt & bind

Layer quilt top on batting and backing and quilt the way you like. Square up all raw edges.

Cut (8) 2½" strips from binding fabric. Piece together end-to-end with diagonal seams, aka *the plus sign method*.

Fold in half lengthwise, press. Attach to your quilt raw edges together with a ¼" seam.

Turn the folded binding edge to the back and tack in place with an invisible stitch or machine stitch if you like.

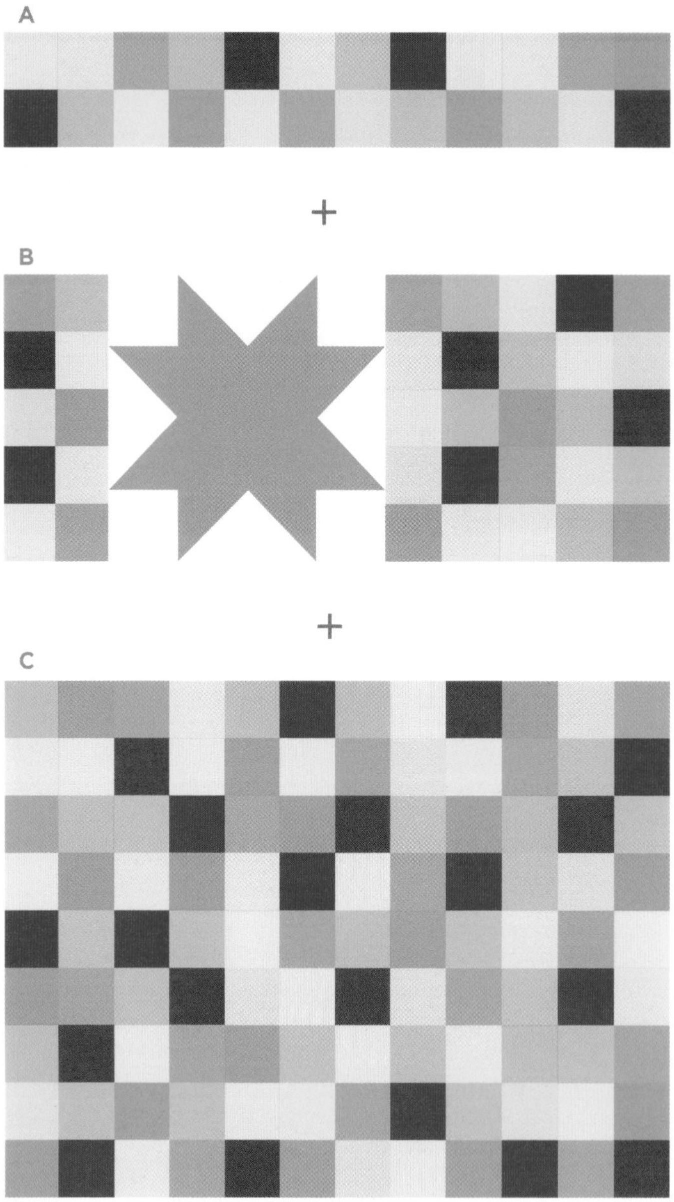

2 sew charm squares together in 3 sections; press all even rows to one side; odd rows to the other side

3 attach inner border to the top & bottom **A** & **B**; then both sides **C** & **D**; repeat for outer border

Building Memories

quilt designed by JENNY DOAN

Traveling is difficult when you have a lot of children. (Heck, what's not difficult with a lot of children?) But spending time together was always a priority, so for us, camping fit the bill. We absolutely loved to camp, and so many of my favorite memories are colored by the smell of our old canvas tent and the taste of pancakes cooked on a propane stove.

On these trips, we usually stuck to our trusty tent and sleeping bags, but one summer we had a chance to stay in a friend's log cabin. Our kids thought it was the most amazing vacation they'd ever had! And I have to admit, I fell in love too. There is so much peace to be had in a log cabin; It was undeniably homey and seemed to transport us back in time to a simpler way of life. When the trip was over, none of us wanted to leave.

Making a log cabin quilt is another way to connect to that peace and simplicity. It's a classic pattern dating back centuries that I feel really ties us to our history. The center square is traditionally either red, to represent the heart of the home, or yellow, to represent a welcoming candlelit window. That symbolism adds extra meaning to a pattern that already means a lot to me.

You see, the log cabin quilt is the first quilt I ever made. Years ago (I won't admit how many), I took a community class on Eleanor Burns Quilt in a Day. I had a great time, as you may have guessed, and it really lit a fire under me. I also realized that I could take the log cabin blocks and simply rotate them to create whole new patterns. I was absolutely smitten. I've been called enthusiastic, and I suppose it's true, because by the end of the class I had made twelve quilts!

I guess I like to give life everything I've got, whether that means making twelve quilts where only one was expected, or roughing it with my crazy family in a tent! Although, of course, if I get the chance, next time it will be a log cabin.

JENNY AND RON POSE WITH THE FOUR YOUNGEST DOAN KIDS. The beach is a great place to go when your raising a large family on a budget! We spent many wonderful hours combing the rocks, shores, and tidepools for interesting bits of treasure.

"Making a log cabin quilt is another way to connect to that peace and simplicity."

materials

makes a 80″ x 80″ honey bun & jelly roll quilt

QUILT TOP
- 1 jelly roll print
- 1 honey bun solid
- 1½ yd outer border

BINDING
- ¾ yd coordinating fabric

BACKING
- 6¾ yds 44″ wide OR 2¼ yds 90″ wide

SAMPLE QUILT
- **Incarnadine** by Robyn Pandolph for RJR
- **Cotton Supreme French Vanilla** for RJR

1 cut & sew

Select 3 dark jelly roll strips for the log cabin center. Subcut into (36) 2½″ squares (16/strip).

Attach a 1½″ strip to the center square by using a modified chain piecing method to quickly sew blocks together. Position a 2½″ center square on top of a 1½″ honey bun strip RST, lining up the right edges. Sew ¼″ seam. Take a few stitches beyond the square. Place another 2½″ square and sew it to the strip. Continue in this fashion (16/strip). The sewing machine's needle down position will come in handy. Trim off excess fabric between squares. Press to the square.

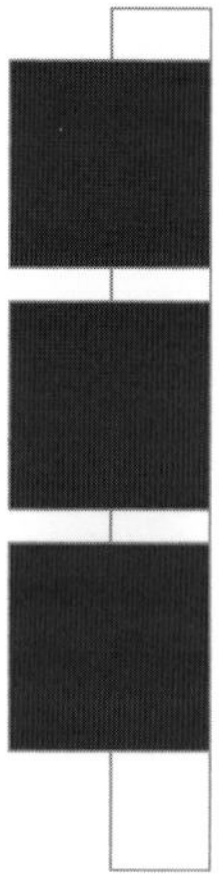

1 use a modified chain piecing method to add strips

***TIP:** Keep a consistent seam allowance throughout. That is your key to success with the log cabin block*

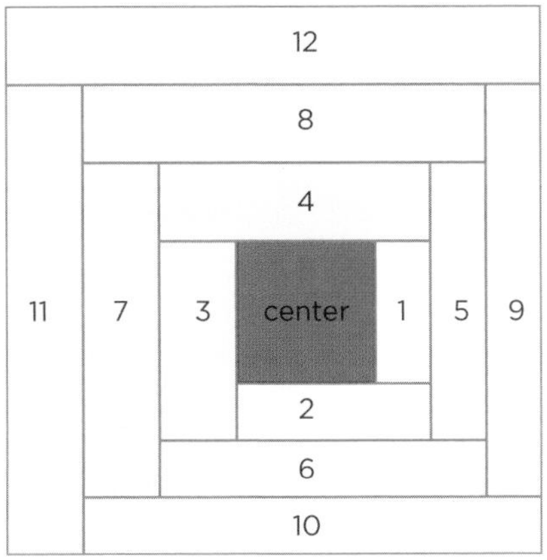

2 construct the log cabin in a circular sequence; 2½″ jelly roll strips are shown in light blue representing prints; honey bun strips are solid white

2 build the block

The log cabin block is constructed using the chain piecing method (discussed above) in the following sequence: starting with strip # 1, add 2 honey bun strips, then 2 jelly roll strips. Each strip is added to the next side around the center square in a spiral path. Repeat 3 times around the center square for a total of 12 strips. Make 36 blocks.

Block size: 11½″ x 11½″

3 arrange & sew

The 36 blocks form a 6 x 6 grid. 2 basic rows of 6 blocks repeat in the quilt: A & B. Build (4) A rows & (2) B rows. Sew blocks together side-to-side across. Press seams in A rows to the same side; in B rows to the opposite side.

Sew 2 sections of 3 rows together: A+B+A. Nest seams as you go. Flip 1 section upside down and sew the sections together to finish the quilt center.

Quilt center size: 66½″ x 66½″

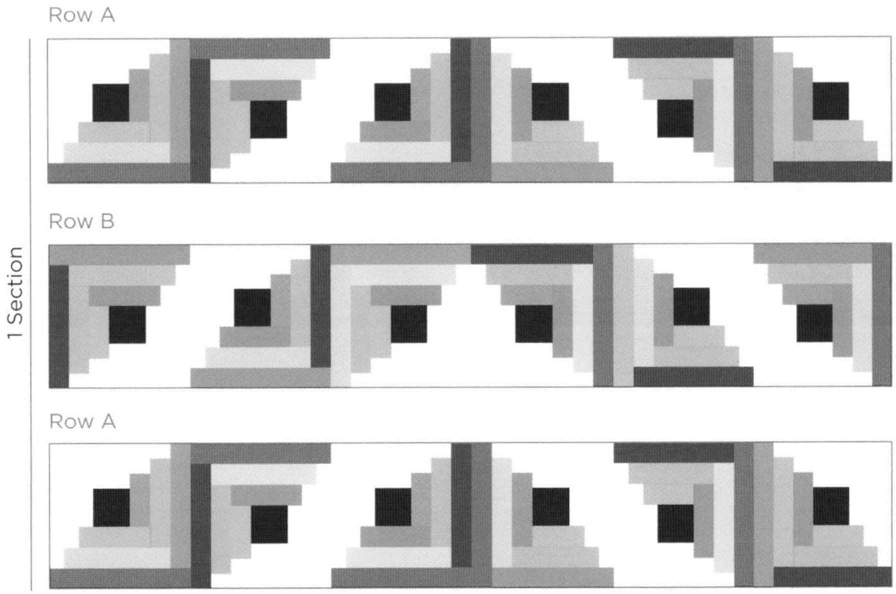

4 borders

Find the average measurement of the quilt width (measure in three places). Piece together 1½″ strips and cut 2 strips to that size. Attach to the top and bottom. Borders A & B Press to the borders.

Repeat for the sides measuring lengthwise. Include the newly attached borders in your measurements. Piece strips together and cut 2 strips to that length. Attach 1 border to each side. C & D Press to the borders.

Cut (8) 6″ strips of outer border fabric. Attach to the quilt in the same manner as the inner border.

5 quilt & bind

Layer quilt top on batting and backing and quilt the way you like. Square up all raw edges.

Cut (8) 2½″ strips from binding fabric. Piece together end-to-end with diagonal seams, aka *the plus sign method*.

Fold in half lengthwise, press. Attach to your quilt raw edges together with a ¼″ seam.

Turn the folded binding edge to the back and tack in place with an invisible stitch or machine stitch if you like.

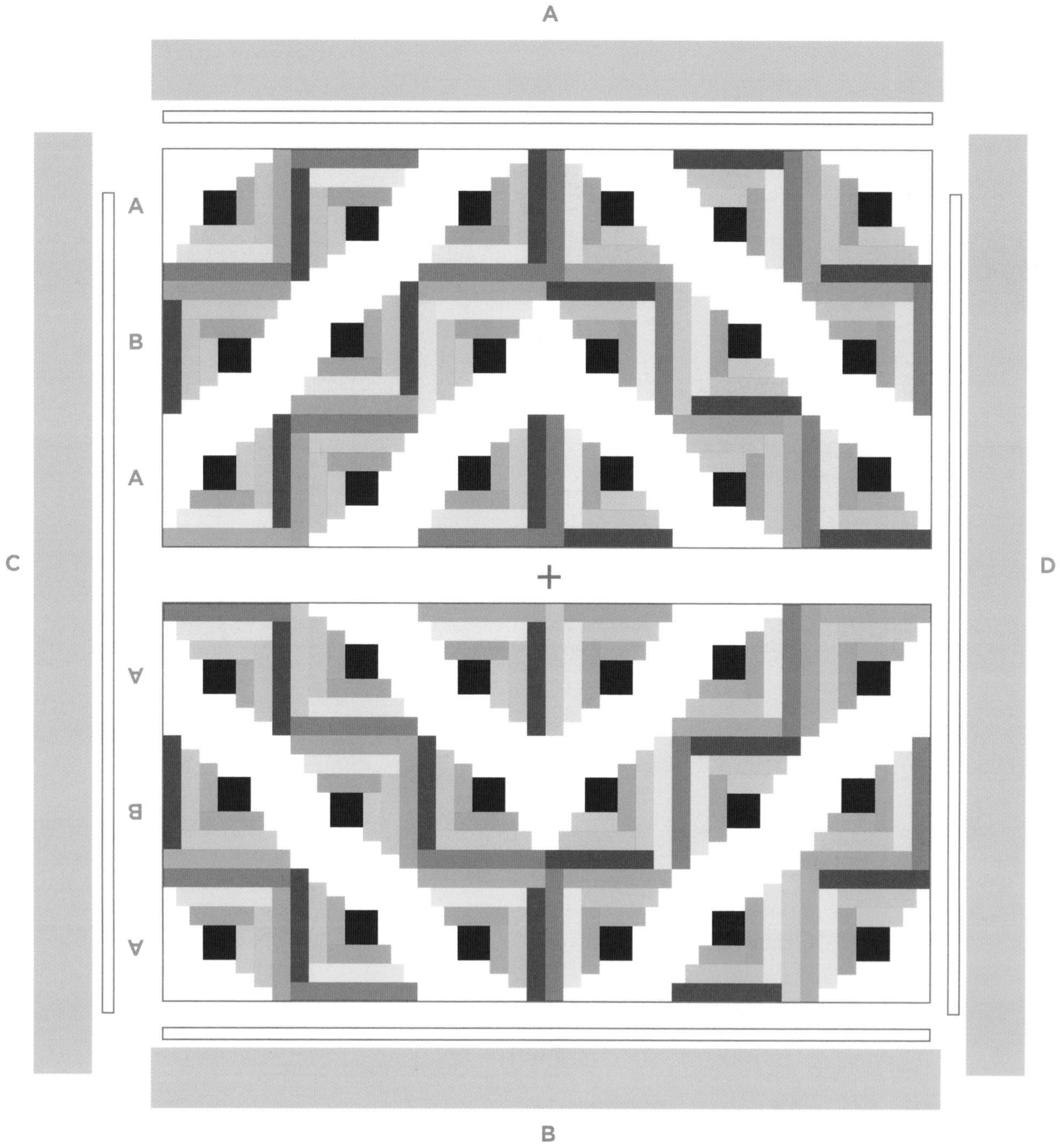
A
A
B
A
C
+
D
A
B
A
B

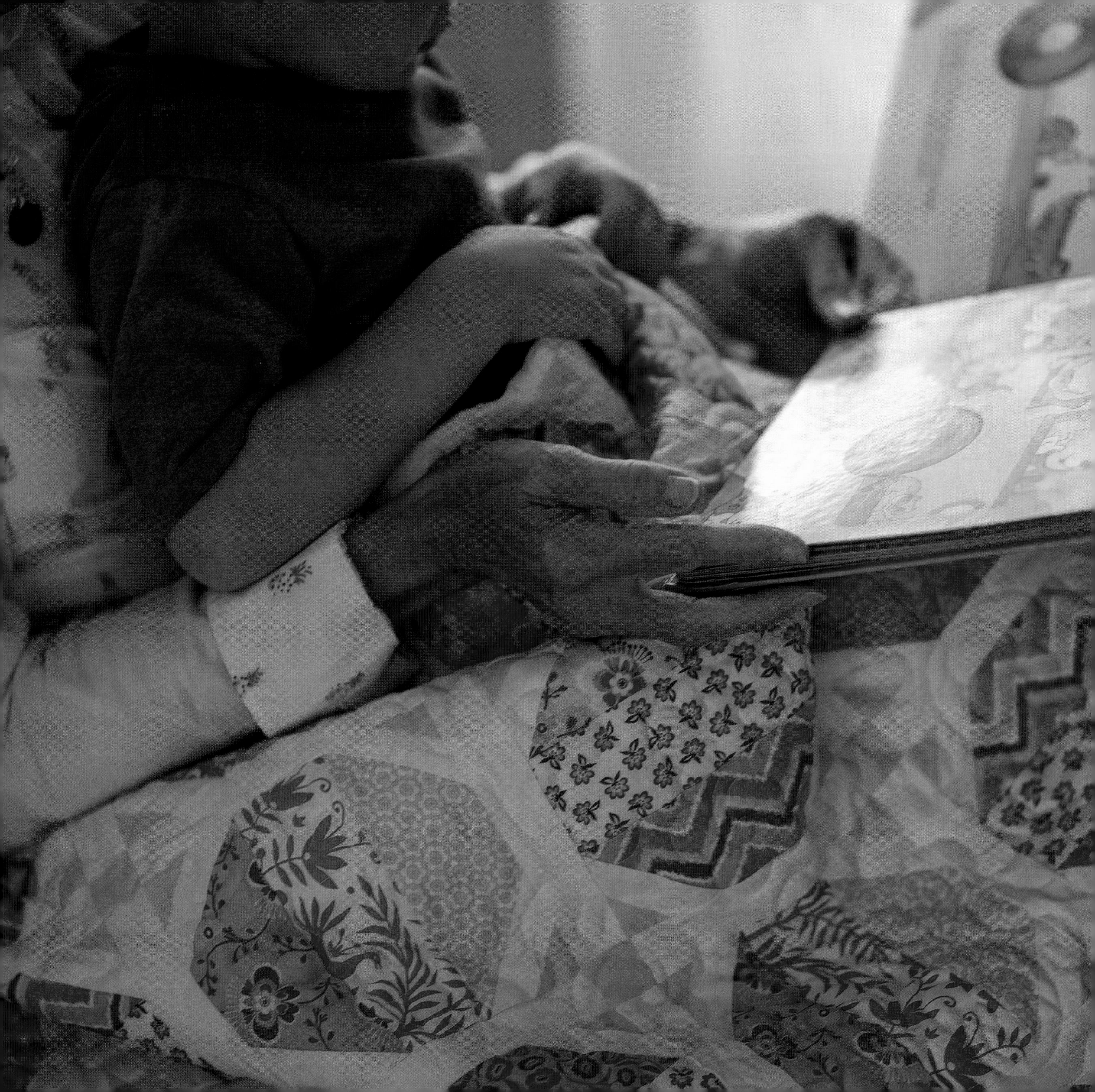

What you wish for

quilt designed by JENNY DOAN

My grandmother was an endlessly practical woman, but ironic as it may seem, she was also decidedly superstitious. She taught me to save scraps, eat leftovers, and wear hand-me-downs, but she is also the person that instilled in me an irrepressible urge to throw salt over my shoulder every time it's spilled.

Having survived the Great Depression, Grandma knew how to pinch a penny, and she certainly wasn't one to waste money. Still, there was one cause for which she always had a coin: the wishing well.

There was a small fountain outside the public library in town. Grandma and I shared a love of reading, so she took me to the library often. In all those many years, we never passed the fountain without Grandma handing me a penny to toss into the water and saying, "Make a wish," before she dropped one in herself.

"... as the rules for wishes go, telling your wish means it won't come true ..."

I always wondered what Grandma was wishing for when she dropped her penny in, but I must admit I was a bit too shy to ask. Anyway, I figured she wouldn't tell me even if I did ask because, as the rules for wishes go, telling your wish means it won't come true, right? Was she wishing for money? Financial security to leave her memories of want firmly behind? A bigger home or fancy car? I really doubted that. Now as an adult I imagine she might have wished for her children to be safe and successful, (or maybe even for some yardage to add to her fabric stash!).

A couple of years before Grandma passed, I took my children to her home for a visit. We sat in the yard in the shade of her favorite oak tree and watched the kids chase a soccer ball around the lawn. Grandma held my littlest one in her lap. We talked about babies, families, the past, and the future. I don't know if Grandma was thinking of our trips to the library fountain or not, but that afternoon as she snuggled the baby against her chest, she smiled at the squealing soccer players and told me with a wink that she had gotten everything she had ever wished for.

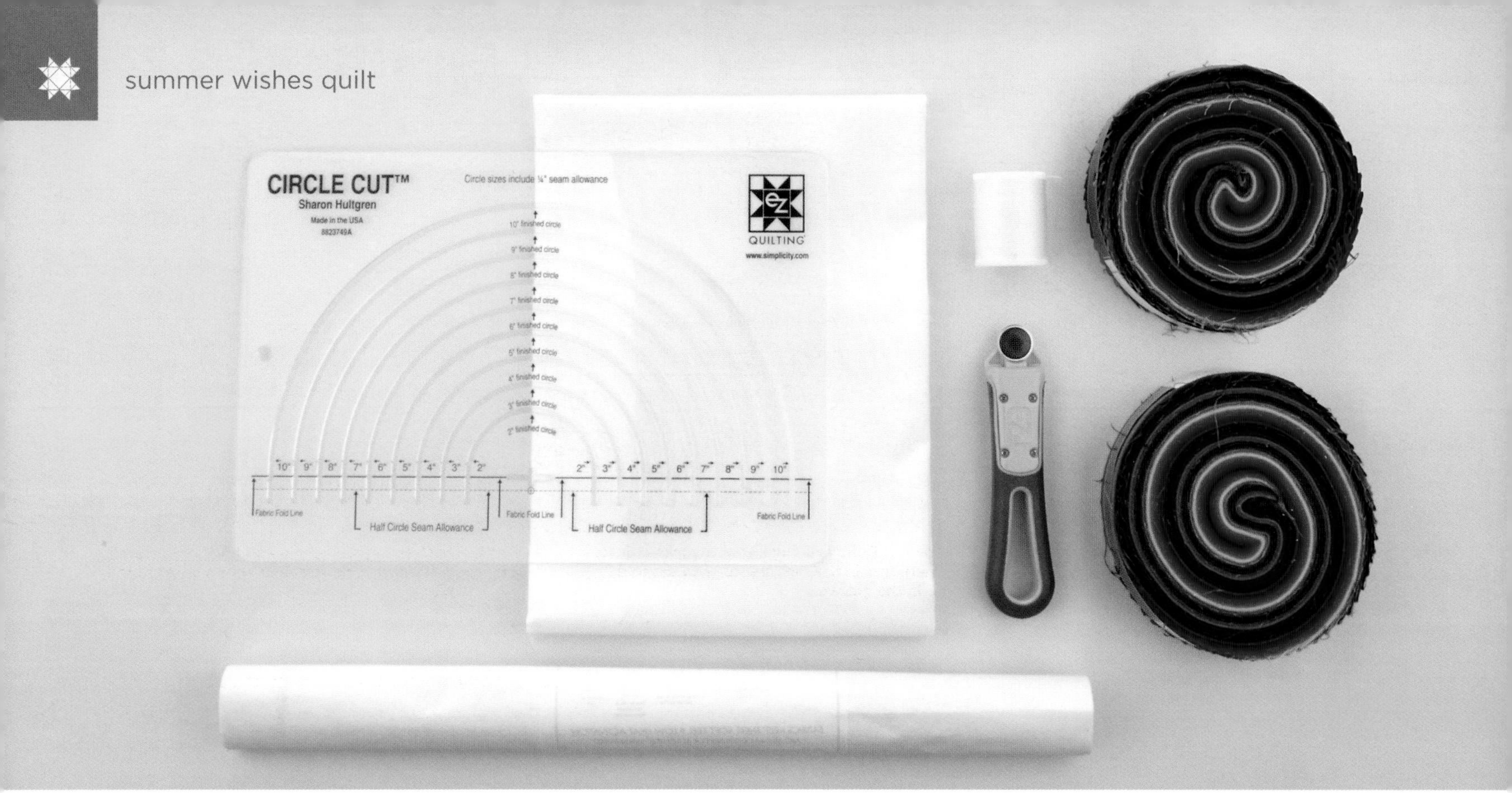

materials

makes a 71" X 91" honey bun quilt

QUILT TOP

- 2 honey buns
- 4½ yds background fabric

OTHER TOOLS

- Easy Circle Cut Ruler
- Heat 'n Bond
- 18mm rotary cutter
- Quilt Basting Spray

BINDING

- ¾ yd coordinating fabric

BACKING

- 5½ yds 44" wide **OR** 2¼ yds 108" wide

SAMPLE QUILT

- **Kona Classic Collection** for Robert Kaufman
- **Bella Solids Bleached White** (98) for Moda

1 sew & cut

Select 10 honey bun strips of various colors and sew RST lengthwise. Be consistent with your seam allowance. Make 8 strip sets. Press all seams to one side.

Measure the width of your strip sets. Use that measurement to subcut the strip sets into blocks. For our purposes, we will assume a 10½" width. If your size is different, cut to that size. The most important thing is the blocks are square.

Yield: (32) 10½" x 10½" blocks

IMPORTANT TIP: *the blocks should all be the same size and square.*

1 make 8 strip sets of 10 honey bun strips; subcut into 32 squares

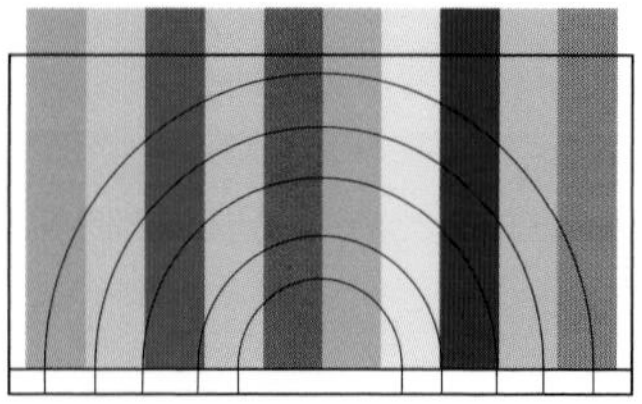

2 cut out circles

1 Measure the width of your strip set. Subcut to that size creating squares. (For our purposes we use 10½")

2 The Easy Cut Ruler is a quick way to make cirlces. Fold the blocks in half, line the ruler to the fold, and cut in the groove.

3 Each honey bun circle and honey bun block without a circle is paired with a background block.

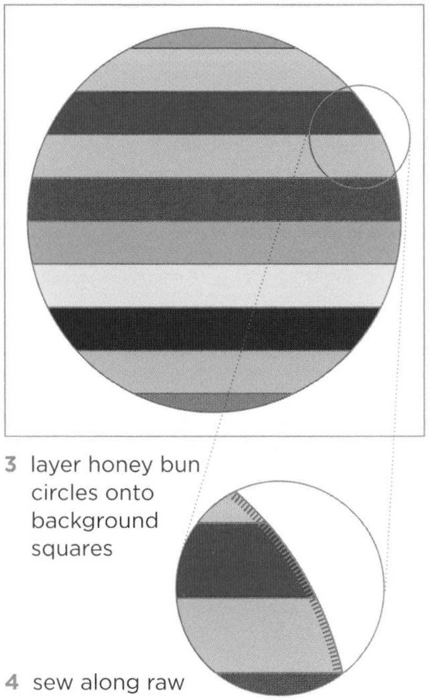

3 layer honey bun circles onto background squares

4 sew along raw edges of the circle

2 make circles

Use the *Easy Cut Circle Ruler* and a small 18mm rotary cutter in this step. Fold a honey bun block in half. Place the ruler's guideline along the folded edge and cut using the *8" finished* half circle groove. This makes an 8½" circle.

Yield: (32) circles &
(32) blocks without a center

3 build the blocks

From the background yardage cut 16 strips to the same width size of your blocks. For our purposes we use 10½." Subcut each strip into (4) 10" blocks (or the size of your block).

Yield: (64) 10½" x 10½" background blocks

Optional: spray the backs of all the honey bun blocks & circles with fabric adhesive or use Heat 'n Bond in this step.

Layer all honey bun blocks without a center AND honey bun circles onto a background block. Position the circles by eyeballing it. Or you can finger press the center in both the background and the circle and match those centers with a pin. Pin in place if no spray adhesive or Heat 'n Bond is used. Make 64 blocks.

4 sew

Stitch around the circle's—or missing circle's—raw edge with a zig-zag, straight or blanket stitch.

5 arrange & sew

Lay out 63 blocks in a 7 x 9 grid. Alternate white circle, honey bun circle across in rows and from row to row. There will be 1 block leftover.

Begin sewing in the top left corner. Sew all blocks together side-to-side to make rows.

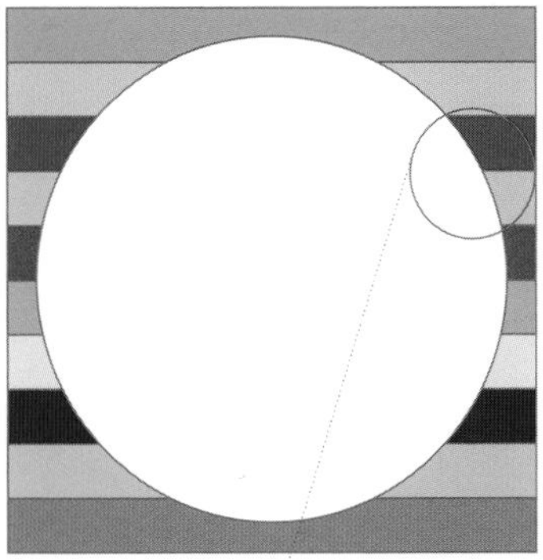

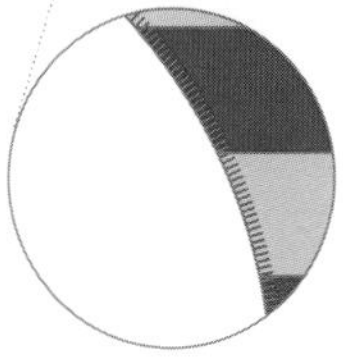

3 layer honey bun blocks without circles onto background squares

4 sew along raw edges of the honey bun block

Press seams of even rows to one side; seams of odd rows to the opposite side. This will make nesting seams a breeze. Sew all rows together to make the quilt center, nesting seams as you go.

Quilt center size: 70½" x 90½" *(based on 10½" blocks)*

6 quilt & bind

Layer quilt top on batting and backing and quilt the way you like. Square up all raw edges.

Cut (9) 2½" strips from binding fabric. Piece together end-to-end with diagonal seams, aka *the plus sign method*.

Fold in half lengthwise, press. Attach to your quilt raw edges together with a ¼" seam.

Turn the folded binding edge to the back and tack in place with an invisible stitch or machine stitch if you like.

5 Keep all the stripes in the blocks horizontal

Lucky penny
a hexagon quilt

quilt designed by SHEA HENDERSON

Summertime is the perfect time to play outside. Dreary skies, make way for sunshine! I'm ready to close the door on washing my dishes and pack up the family to hit the baseball fields, bike trails, or anything else that takes us out into the open air!

My kids and I often spent mornings inside working on school or projects. Even in the spring, life kept us busy! Afternoons were our free time. A favorite activity was penny walks.

In a penny walk, one gathers everyone up and heads outside with no particular destination, walks to the corner, and flips a coin to find out where you'll be going. Heads - you turn right. Tails - you turn left. If you catch it or drop it, you go straight. (That last one sometimes changed depending on the skill of the child flipping the coin.)

OUR LIVES ARE LIKE QUILTS - bits and pieces, joy and sorrows, stitched together with love.

A little flexibility in your plans might be required, but you find the greatest treasures when you're out exploring your own town. We've discovered beautiful gardens, made new friends, and found new places to play. Our penny walks were a great way to get everyone outside and together. Aside from a few directional vetoes, they also made for a nice, meandering walk—sometimes around the block, sometimes across town.

As quilters, we love a new take on an old quilt, and this little hexagon quilt is just that. With a touch of flexibility and a charm pack or two, there's always something new to be sewn up.

“ A little flexibility in your plans might be required, but you find the greatest treasures when you’re out exploring your own town. ”

materials

makes a 47" X 58" charm pack quilt

QUILT TOP
- 2 charm packs print
- 2 charm packs background solid
- ½ yd outer border

BINDING
- ½ yd coordinating fabric

BACKING
- 3¼ yds 44" wide **OR**
- 1½ yds 90" wide

SAMPLE QUILT
- **Up Parasol** by Heather Bailey for Free Spirit
- **Bella Solids Snow** (11) by Moda

1 cut

Of the print charm squares you will need all but 12. Cut out the half hexie shape from all the charm squares—prints and solids. If you have a rotating cutting mat or small mat that you can pick up and turn, you may want to use it here.

You can experiment with the order you cut. It may be easier to cut the charm square in half first, stack the rectangles, then trim out the half hexie. Or, you can fold the charm square, cut out the shape, open the fold, and cut the fold line. It's up to you. Keep any print charms paired up once they've been cut. It will be easier to assemble the quilt if you do.

1 cut out 2 half hexie shape from folded or cut charm squares; keep print halves stacked together

2A this layout repeats 3 times across in rows 1 & 3; in rows 2 & 4 the triangles point in the opposite direction;

1 Use the half hexie ruler to cut a folded charm square. Or, cut all the charm squares in half first and then cut out the shape.

2 The half hexies are joined along their slanted edges. Once the seam is sewn they will form a straight strip.

3 The first & last background hexie of each row is cut in half, a quarter hexie!

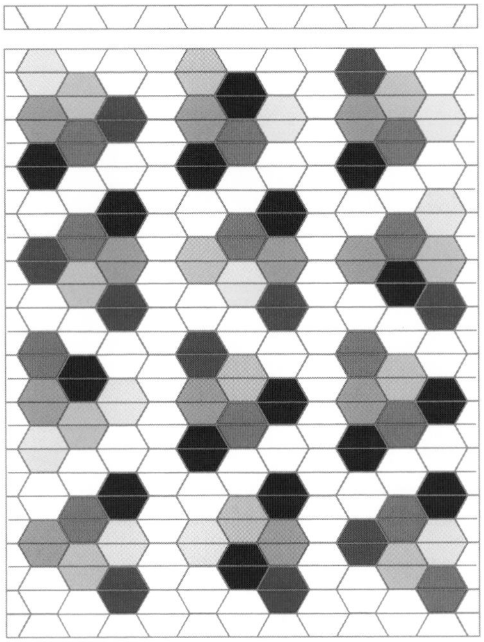

2B add 1 row of white half hexies top & bottom; then add a column of white quarter hexies to both sides

3A & B build rows first, then sew them together

2 arrange

Layout the entire quilt in a 13 x 26 grid *before* sewing. The basic "triangle" block is shown in **2A** (6 print full hexagons + 6 white half hexies). Note that print pairs match along the widest side. Lay out 3 triangles per row. Make 4 rows. In rows 1 & 3, triangles point right; in rows 2 & 4, triangles point left. Add a column of white half hexies between each triangle in every row. Add a row of white half hexies to the top and bottom.

Of the remaining white half hexies cut 13 in half. These quarter hexies are placed at the beginning and end of each row.

3 sew

First construct the rows. There are 13 elements to a row, and 26 rows. Start at the top left corner. Match the slanted sides RST, offsetting the 2 half hexies at the ¼" seam line just a smidgen, and sew. **3A** Continue building the row.

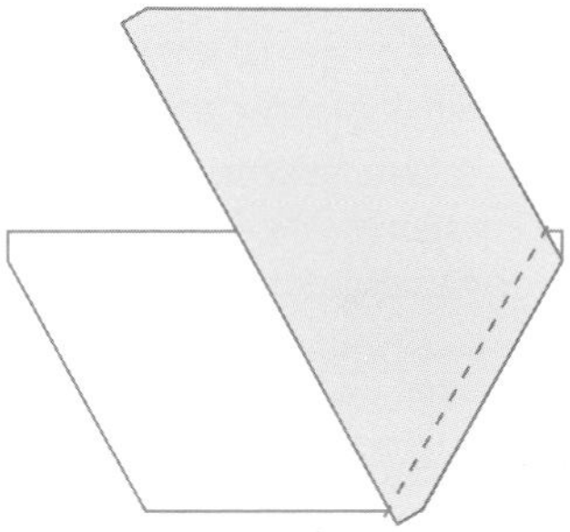

3A RST offset 2 half hexies and sew along the slanted edge; continue down the column

Press all seams in one direction in odd rows; to the opposite direction in even rows. Sew rows together; nest seams. **3B**

Quilt center size: 41½" x 52½"

4 attach outer border

Cut (6) 3" strips of border fabric. Measure the width 3 times. Piece strips as needed to attain the average size and cut 2 strips to that length. Attach 1 to the top, 1 to the bottom. A & B Press to the borders. Repeat for both sides measuring the length and including the borders just attached. C & D

5 quilt & bind

Layer quilt top on batting and backing and quilt the way you like. Square up all raw edges.

Cut (5) 2½" strips from binding fabric. Piece together end-to-end with diagonal seams, aka *the plus sign method.*

Fold in half lengthwise, press. Attach to your quilt raw edges together with a ¼" seam.

Turn the folded binding edge to the back and tack in place with an invisible stitch or machine stitch if you like.

4 attach outer borders

THESE HALF HEXAGON QUILTS ARE A GREAT TWIST on the traditional grandmothers flower garden. They look amazing and stitch together in no time at all!

the apple of my *eye*

quilt designed by JENNY DOAN

America: the land of the free, the home of the brave, and the capital of apple pie! Apple harvest time is a special time for my family, as we gather to make our own home-made canned apple pie filling. You know that stuff you find at the grocery store in a tin can? Don't mention it at my house; it's taboo around here. We're devoted to the home-canned variety: yummier to eat, more fun to make!

When the apples are ripe, I alert the crew. It's time to get down to business—pie filling day is here! We start out picking together. After the first two minutes, picking apples can get tiresome, but I'll tell you what, it's a lot easier to motivate yourself when you know that every apple you pick will end up swimming in spices and snuggled between layers of buttery crust!

Armed with a whole bushel of apples, we settle into the work of peeling, coring, slicing, and canning the yummy

fruit. The grandkids have fun using my crank-operated apple peeler, which expertly strips off the skin in one long coil. We sometimes argue over the exact ratio of cinnamon to nutmeg, but I whip out my old, stained recipe card and lay that matter to rest. The kitchen can get awfully crowded, hot, and sticky, but the smell is pure heaven.

As we finish, it's so satisfying to line up the gleaming bottles full of honey-colored pie filling, still hot from processing. I wouldn't say I love to cook—mostly because the finished product is gobbled up and forgotten in less time than it took to make—but with my bottled pie filling, we get to enjoy the fruits of our labors (pun intended) for months. I know it's silly, but I keep the filling in my pantry right in front where they're on display every time I open the door, just for the smile I get on my face when I see them.

It may be true that not every single sticky moment of the canning process feels magical at the time, but the memories of working together with my family are even sweeter to me than the mouthwatering slice of hot apple pie I'll be savoring come winter!

materials

makes a 62¼" X 69¼" layer cake quilt

QUILT TOP
- 1 layer cake print
- 1¼ yd solid
- 1½ yd outer border

BINDING
- ½ yd coordinating fabric

BACKING
- 4 yds 44" wide **OR** 2 yds 90" wide

ADDITIONAL TOOLS
- MSQC Apple Core layer cake shape
- small **OR** rotating cutting mat

SAMPLE QUILT
- **Everything But the Kitchen Sink** by Yuko Hasegawa for RJR
- **Bella Solids White PDF** (97) by Moda

1 cut

Cut the *Apple Core* shape from all 42 layer cakes. A rotating cutting mat or a small cutting mat that can be picked up and turned is a handy tool for cutting apple cores.

Cut (4) 10" strips from the solid fabric. Subcut into (14) 10" squares. Cut apple core shapes from all of these. Subcut 7 apple cores in half lengthwise; 7 in half widthwise. After laying these out, cut the remaining "half" apple cores in half again to use for the corners.

2 arrange

Lay out the print apple cores into

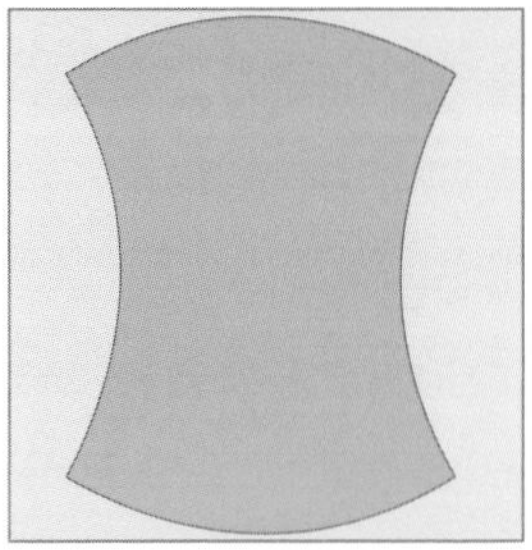

1 cut apple core shapes from layer cakes

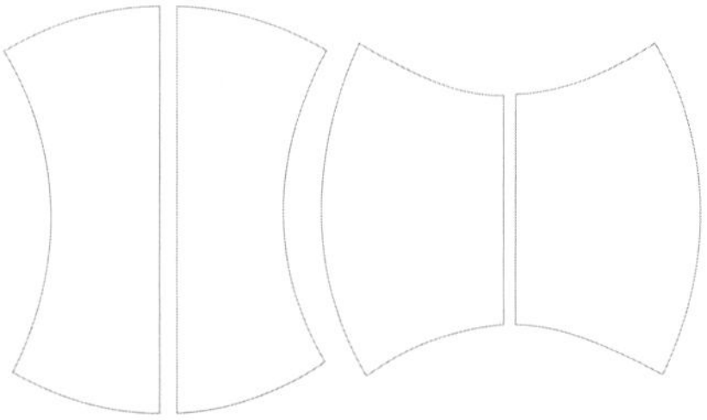

1 7 of the solid apple core shapes will be cut in half lengthwise, 7 in half widthwise

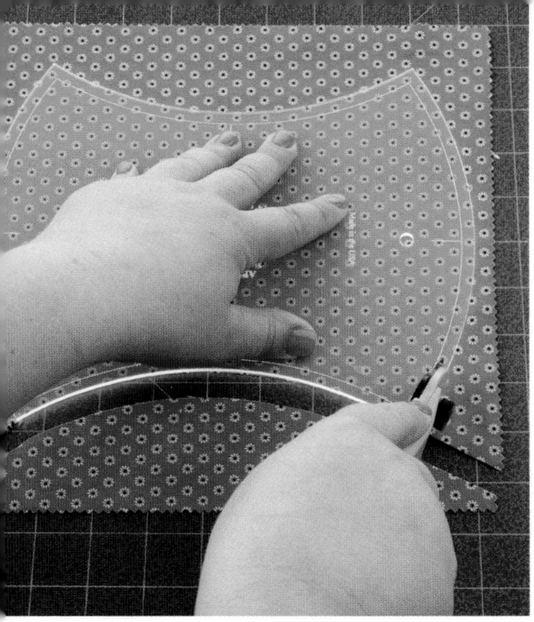

1 Cut apple core shapes from all the print layer cakes.

2 Match the corners. Have the convex shape on top; the concave shape below. Sew to the point at which the raw edges still meet. Stop, realign the edges and continue.

3 Cut 7 solid layer cakes in half widthwise.

4 Cut 7 layer cakes in half lengthwise.

5 After laying out the quilt center there will be 2 solid halves left over. Cut these in half again. They are the corners.

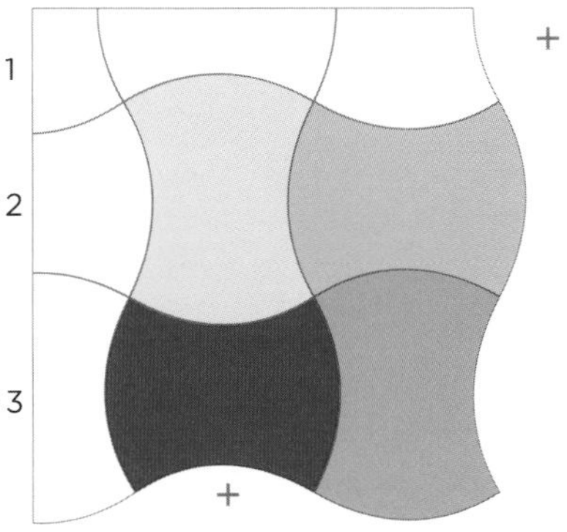

2 layout the blocks matching convex & concave curves

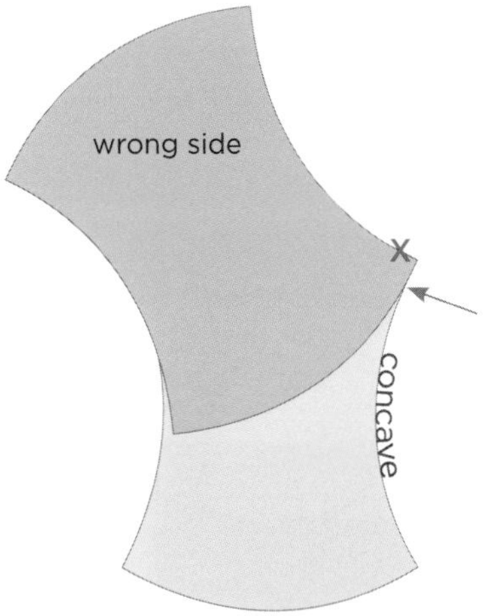

3 sew the curved seam with the concave block on the bottom

a 6 x 7 grid in an eye-pleasing arrangement, matching the convex and concave shapes as you go. Add a "border" of white half apple cores around the perimeter.

3 sew

Sew rows together first. Include the half apple cores as part of the row.

The easiest way to sew the curved seams is to have the concave block on the bottom. This way you will be able to see both fabrics as you line up their raw edges.

Start the ¼" seam at the **X**. Sew to the point where the raw edges still match (see arrow). Stop and realign the edges by gently sliding the top layer over—without pulling—and sew another 4-6 stitches. The "needle down" feature on your sewing machine will come in handy with this type of sewing.

Take your time and keep the fabric flat in front of the needle. Let the layers pucker or bunch up behind or to the side of the needle. Press toward the concave shape.

When sewing rows together nest the seams. *Recommended strategy:* stitch every other block pair that has the concave shape on the bottom; then flip the row over and sew the unfinished block pairs. This will keep the concave curve on the bottom. Press the horizontal seams in one direction.

Quilt center size: 50¾" x 57¾"
(including ½ apple cores)

4 outer border

Square up the quilt center. Cut (7) 6½" strips of outer border fabric. Find the average measurement of the quilt width (measure in three places). Cut 2 strips to that size, piecing strips together when needed. Attach 1 to the top and 1 to the bottom. **A** & **B** Press to the borders.

Repeat for the sides measuring lengthwise. Include the newly attached borders in your measurements. Cut 2 strips to the average length. Attach 1 border to each side. **C** & **D** Press to the borders.

5 quilt & bind

Layer quilt top on batting and backing and quilt the way you like. Square up all raw edges.

Cut (7) 2½" strips from binding fabric. Piece together end-to-end with diagonal seams, aka *the plus sign method*.

Fold in half lengthwise, press. Attach to your quilt raw edges together with a ¼" seam.

Turn the folded binding edge to the back and tack in place with an invisible stitch or machine stitch if you like.

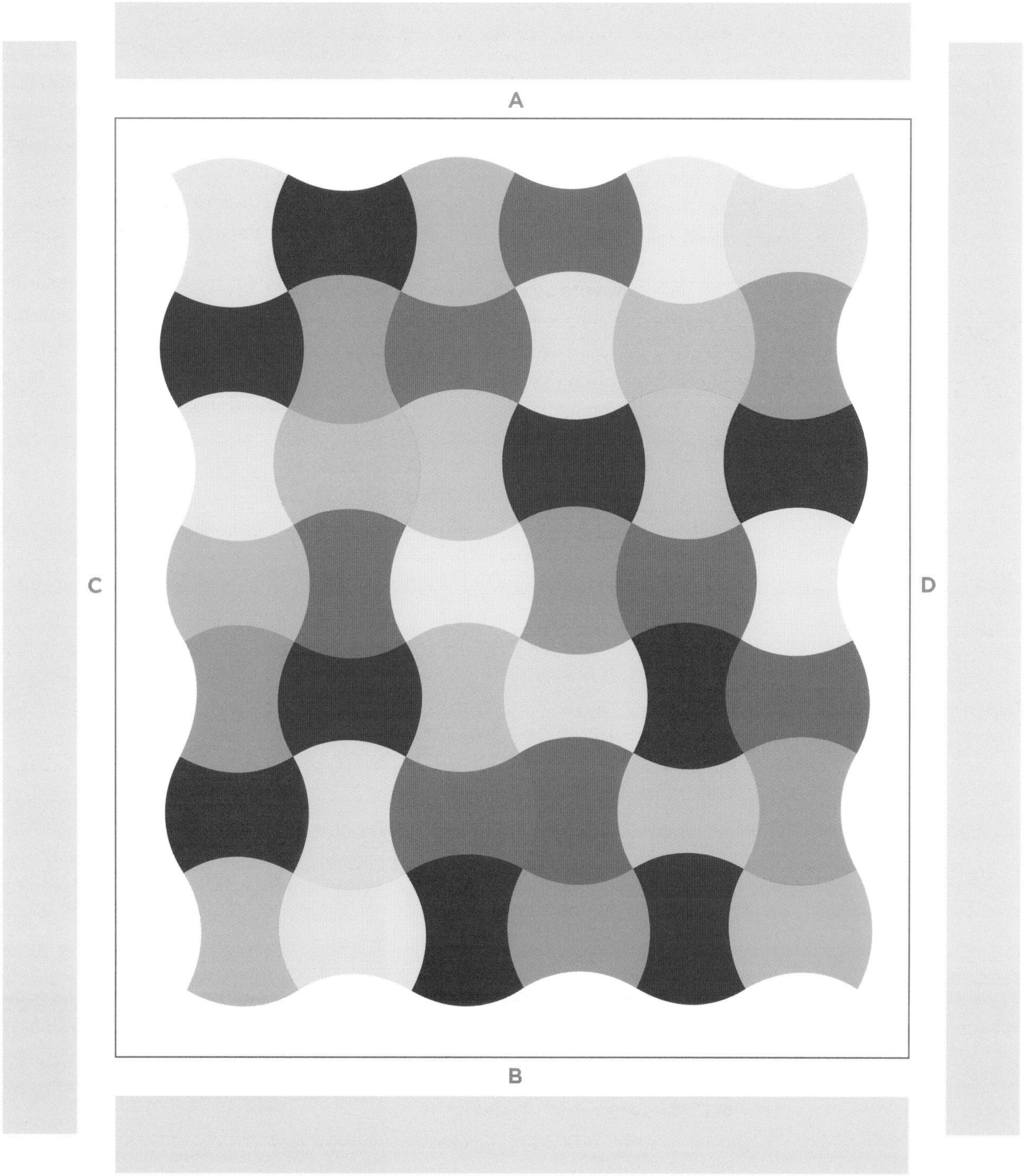
A
B
C
D

Ladies Luncheon

a coin quilt with pizazz

quilt designed by JENNY DOAN

I'm a fan of spontaneous fun. Who needs plans, maps, or reservations when you can improvise with a little imagination? But I have to admit, some things are better with a little preparation and (dare I say it?) a little formality.

For example, when my girls were small—just eight, nine, and ten—my mother hosted a garden party for them. Mom lives by the motto that anything worth doing is worth doing right, and she must have really thought this party was worth doing. Combining the best of her creativity, grandmotherly talents, and flatware, she expertly crafted one of the best memories of my daughters' young lives.

It began when we received formal invitations in the mail. "Why didn't Grandma just ask us when we saw her yesterday?", my eight year-old wanted to know. "This way is fancier," I explained. And

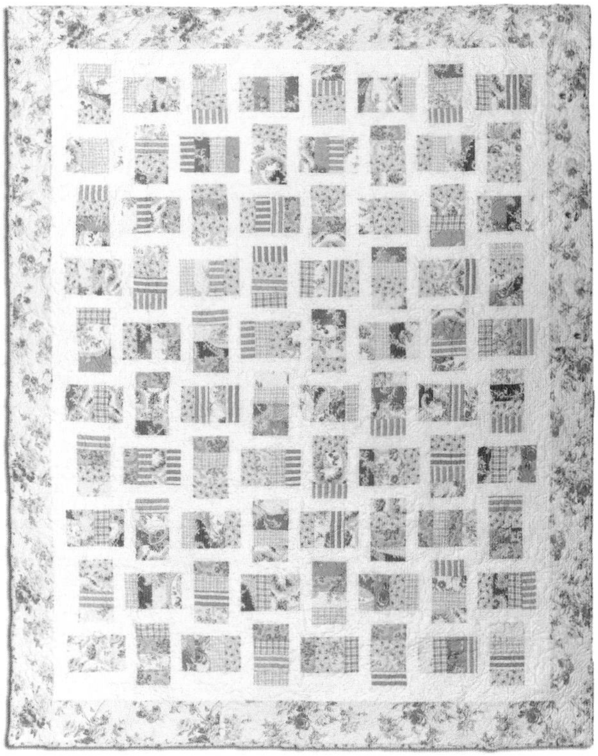

“...each of us has the ability to brighten and beautify our own little corner of the world...”

that was just the beginning. Per Mom's request, we came dressed to the nines, complete with hats and gloves. Mom led us to the back yard, where she had set up a table in the garden. The table was laid with her wedding china and white linen with goblets to drink from, "Just like in the movies," my oldest later said.

The girls were wide-eyed from the beginning. They must have felt as though they had walked into Buckingham Palace. My grandmother was there too, hat and all, bringing four generations of women together at the same table, sharing food and our most refined conversation.

FIVE GENERATIONS OF MOTHERS AND DAUGHTERS. We are so thankful for the time we've spent together and for the memories made.

I'm so grateful the girls got a chance to make this memory, and see all the women in their lives at their most gracious.

They watched us carefully to mirror which fork to use and where to put their hands. Frankly, it was adorable to see them act so proper! The menu was fancy and consisted of food the girls had never heard of, let alone tasted. For a moment I was sure Natalie was going to ask for peanut butter and jelly instead, but at an event this classy she didn't dare complain.

If the girls felt intimidated, that was overshadowed by something they felt even more powerfully. They felt special. They felt like grown-ups. And if you had seen those little sweethearts with lips pursed and pinkies in the air, you would have known, as I did, that this garden party was being locked away into the hearts and memories of those little girls forever.

materials

makes a 78" x 93" charm pack quilt

QUILT TOP
- 4 charm packs
- 3¼ yds sashing & inner border
- 1½ yds outer border

BINDING
- ¾ yd coordinating fabric

BACKING
- 7½ yds 44" wide **OR** 2½ yds 108" wide

SAMPLE QUILT
- **Rosewater** by Verna Mosquera for Free Spirit Fabrics

- **Bella Solids PFD** (97) by Moda Fabrics

1 cut & sew

Cut all the squares of the 4 charm packs in half once.
Yield: 2½" x 5" rectangles.

Sew 2 rectangles together lengthwise RST. Chain piecing will speed up the process. Sew past the fabric a few stitches then place the next pair under the pressure foot and continue through all rectangles. Clip threads and repeat to make 4-strip blocks. Automatic needle down control is a great help when chain piecing.

Avoid all darks or all lights in a single block. Aim for variety as a rule of thumb. Press all seams of a block in the same direction.

Yield: (80) 4-strip blocks *(4 leftovers)*
Block size: 5" x 8½"

2 sashing

From sashing/inner border yardage cut (40) 2¼" strips.

Use a modified form of chain piecing in this step. At the sewing machine, lay a 2¼" sashing strip face up ready to sew lengthwise. Place a 4-strip block face down on top RST, lining up the right edge. Check the block orientation. Sew along the 8½" length, across all four of the block's strips. Make a ¼" seam. A few stitches past the first block, set the next block into position and so on, leaving a bit of a gap.

Yield: 4 blocks per strip.

1 strip set block 5″ x 8½″

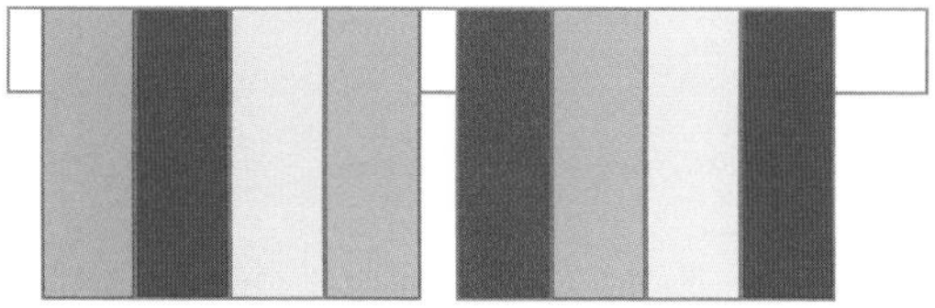

2 add sashing

2 block with sashing

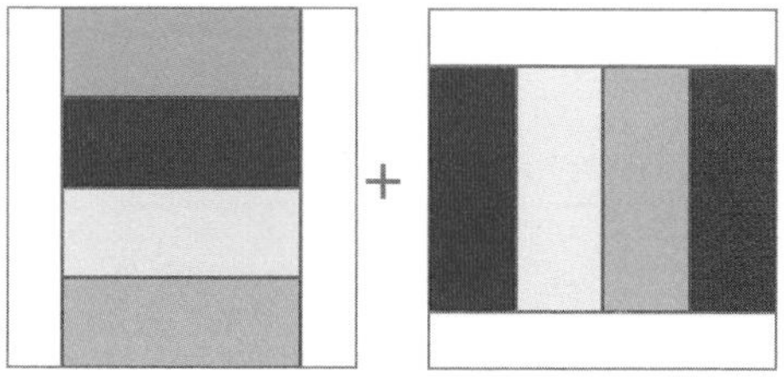

3 horizontal, vertical

TIP: In step 2 sashing is added to both 8½″ sides of the block without additional subcutting. It's a modified chain piecing method. ***Note:*** *Sashing is 2¼″ wide!*

Cut the strip sets apart, trimming sashing as you go. Press to the sashing. Repeat for the opposite side of the block.

Block size: 8½″ x 8½″

3 arrange & sew

Select your blocks and arrange in an 8 x 10 grid alternating the block orientation of vertical, horizontal, vertical, horizontal. Here's where a design wall comes in handy, but a floor or large table does the trick too!

Sew blocks together side to side to make rows. Press seams in one direction for an entire row; in the opposite direction for the following row. This will make nesting the seams a snap when rows are sewn together. Sew rows together to make the center.

Quilt center size: 64½″ x 80½″

4 borders

Cut (8) 2½″ strips of sashing/inner border fabric. Take the average measurement of the quilt's width. Cut 2 strips to that size, piecing the strips when needed. Stitch 1 strip to the top; 1 to the bottom RST. A & B Press to the borders.

Repeat for the sides—this time measuring lengthwise. Include the newly attached borders in your measurements. C & D Press to the borders.

For the outer border cut (9) 5″ strips. Attach in the same manner as the inner border.

5 quilt & bind

Layer quilt top on batting and backing and quilt the way you like. Square up all raw edges.

Cut (9) 2½″ strips of binding and piece together end-to-end with diagonal seams, aka *plus sign method*. Fold in half lengthwise, press. Attach to your quilt, raw edges together with a ¼″ seam allowance.

Turn the folded binding edge to the back and tack in place with an invisible stitch or machine stitch if you like.

TIP: if you are not sewing across seam allowances, you are sewing sashing to the wrong side of the block. Check the orientation of the block.

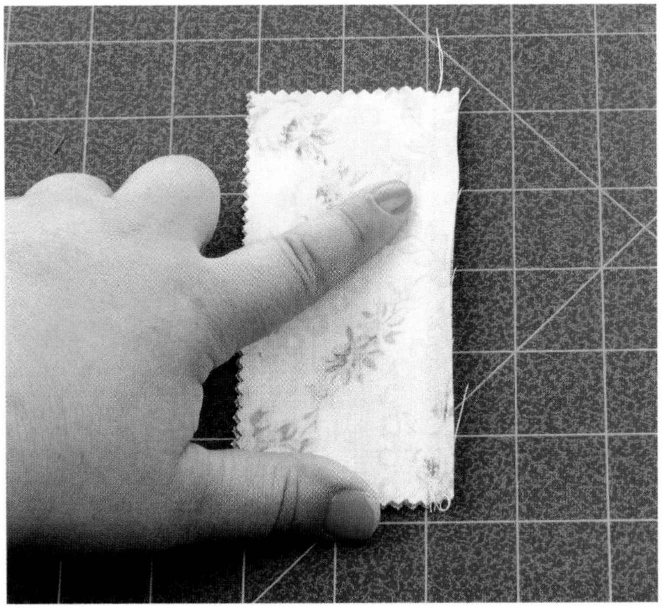

1 Chain piece all the half charm squares into pairs.

2 Chain piece the pairs into a 4-strip set.

3 The 2¼" sashing is added to the longer 8½" side.

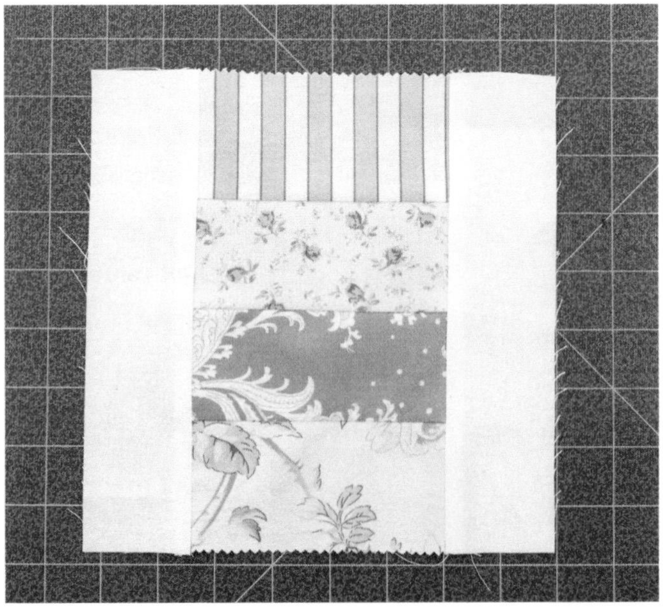

4 The finished block measures 8½" square.

3 arrange & sew
4 add borders

TIP: *Follow the instructions about borders in construction basics to help your quilt remain straight and square.*

How to make a tea towel apron

An apron is a beautiful thing! As long as I can remember, my mom and grandma wore aprons at home, especially while making dinner or doing dishes. My mom's apron slipped over the shoulders and tied at the sides, and Grandma's was embellished with beautiful embroidered flowers. I love the memories I have of these sweet ladies.

On my back porch there is a hook that is full to the brim with cute aprons. When we get together as a family, anyone and everyone puts on an apron and the fun begins. The motto around our house is "Many hands make light work," and I believe that is true! We wear the aprons when cooking, cleaning, canning, or doing any number of arts and craft projects! Every apron gets to do its job and all the family members have a task that is just right for them!

When my Granddaughter Katelyn turned ten, she wanted a party with her friends. She requested a fun project to make and we picked the tea towel apron. We had the girls make cute little cupcake cutouts that they ironed onto the aprons, and then they sewed little buttons onto each cupcake to make the cherry on top! If you could see the smiles on their little faces, you would have thought these girls had won the lottery. This project is ideal for beginners and experienced sewers. Not only are your embellishment options limitless, but these aprons are simple to make and finish up in no time! Enjoy!

apron

A prepare casing: measure 4″ over from center fold; 10″ down from top; press a foldline between those 2 points; cut 1″ from fold line

B finish casing: turn raw edge under ¼,″ press; stitch to apron to form ¾″ casing; thread apron ties up through one side; down through the other

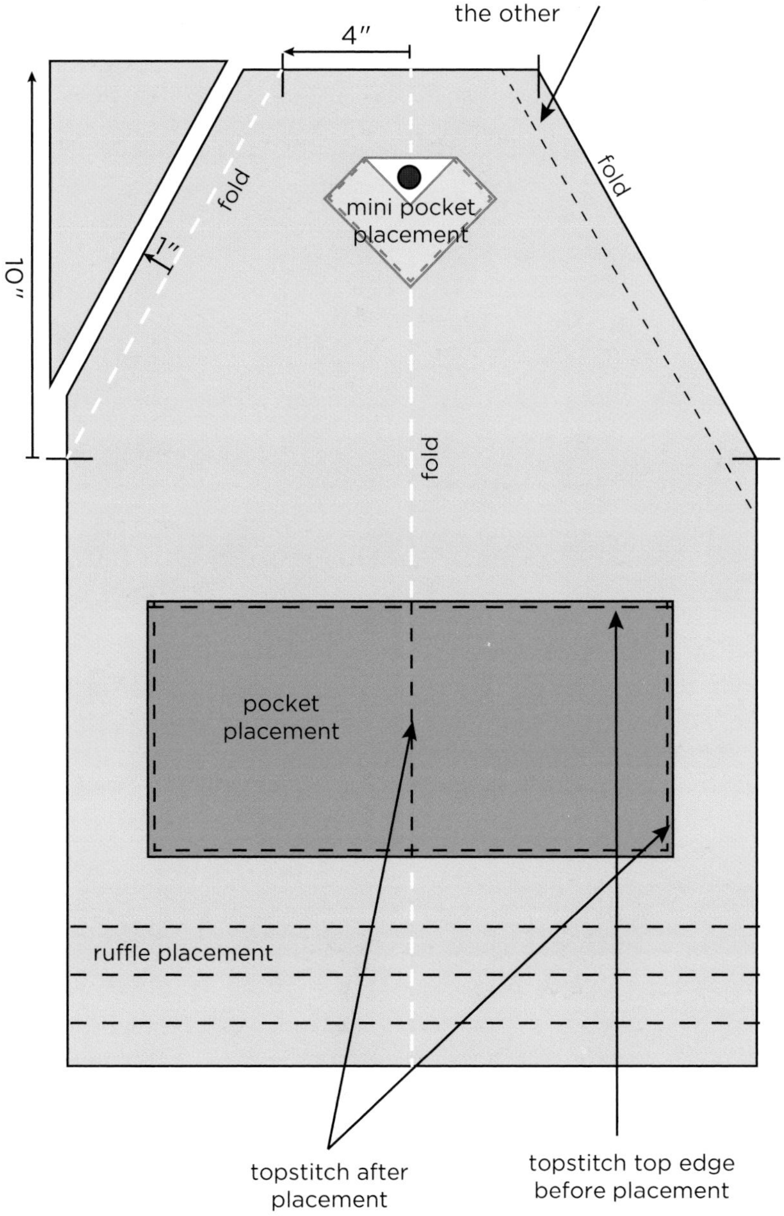

apron ties

C ties: (2-3) 2½″ strips pieced with diagonal seams & pressed open; **3A** finish the ends; topstitch **3B**

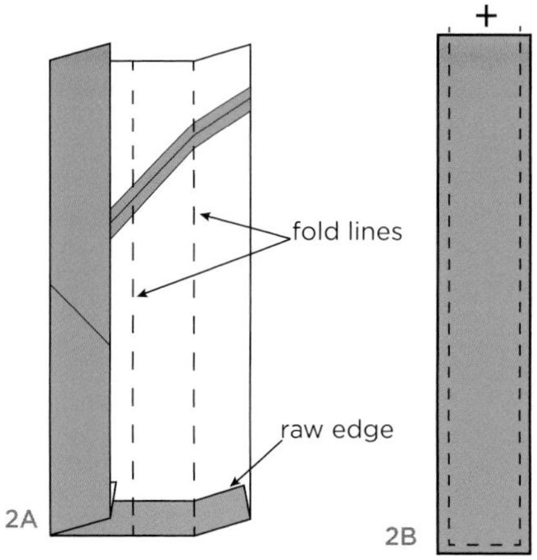

materials

- 1 tea towel (approx size 18″ x 28″)
- (2-3) 2½″ strips for apron ties

OPTIONAL

- (1) 8″ x WOF strip for large pocket
- (2-3) 2½″ strips for ruffles
- 2 charm squares for mini pocket

ONLINE TUTORIAL

msqc.co/174a & msqc.co/174b

apron options:
add a ruffle or pocket

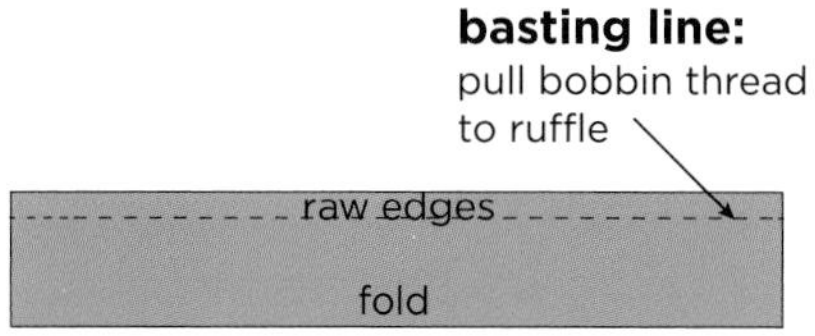

raw-edged ruffle option:
2½″ strip: sew onto apron along basting line after ruffling.

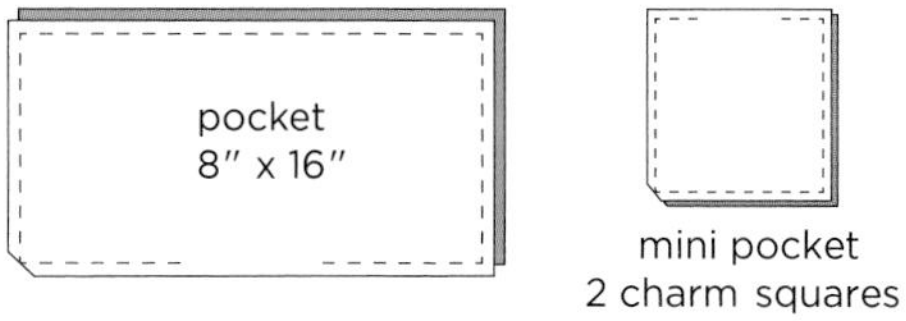

american classic

QUILT SIZE
55" X 64"

DESIGNED BY
Hillary Sperry

PIECED BY
Shea Henderson

QUILTED BY
Jamey Stone

SAMPLE QUILT
Bella Solids White
(98) by Moda
Bella Solids Admiral Blue
(48) by Moda

ONLINE TUTORIALS
msqc.co/american

QUILTING
Loops & Swirls

Quilt	Size	Charm Pack white	Charm Pack blue	Yardage White	Yardage Blue	Binding	Backing
Table Runner	14 x 46	none	none	½ yd	¾ yd	½ yd	1 yd
Throw	55 x 64	1	1	1¼ yd	1¼ yd	½ yd	3½ yds
Queen	73 x 91	2	2	2 yd	2 yd	¾ yd	5½ yds or 2¼ yds 108" wide

NOTE: pattern is written for the quilt size highlighted in this chart.

bloom & grow

QUILT SIZE
28½" X 38½"

DESIGNED BY
Jenny Doan

PIECED BY
Jenny Doan

QUILTED BY
Jamey Stone

QUILT TOP
1 charm pack prints
(1) 2½" strip for stems & leaves
(2) 10" layer cakes for pot
¾ yd background

BINDING
½ yd coordinating fabric

BACKING
1 yd coordinating fabric

ADDITIONAL TOOLS
10" Tumbler shape
Layer Cake Dresden Plate Ruler

SAMPLE QUILT
Windham Basic Brights
by Windham

ONLINE TUTORIALS
msqc.co/bloom

QUILTING
Little Nature

ladies luncheon

QUILT SIZE
78" x 93"

DESIGNED BY
Jenny Doan

PIECED BY
Cassie Nixdorf

QUILTED BY
Cassie Martin

SAMPLE QUILT
Rosewater by Verna Mosquera for Free Spirit Fabrics
Bella Solids PFD (97) by Moda Fabrics

ONLINE TUTORIALS
msqc.co/ladiesluncheon

QUILTING
Just Roses

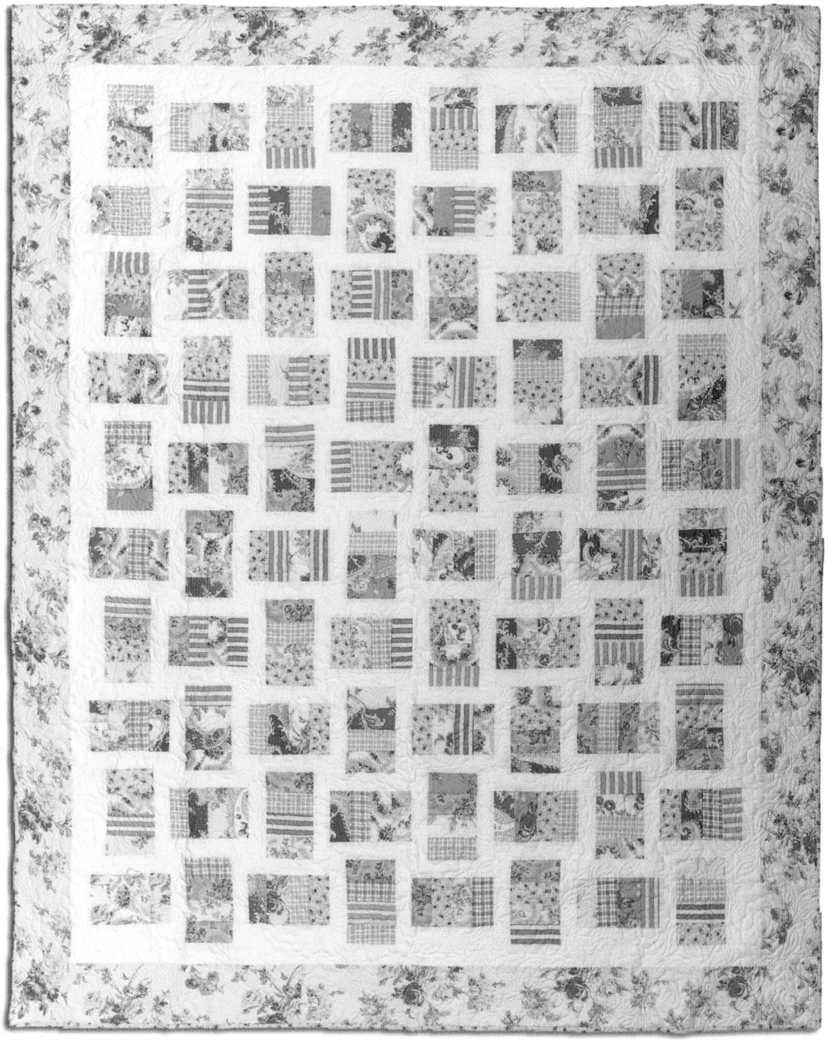

Quilt	Size	Charm Packs	Sashing & Inner Border	Outer Border	Binding	Backing
Table Runner*	21 x 53	1	¾ yd	none	½ yd	1¾ yds
Twin	54 x 78	2	1¼ yds	1 yd	½ yd	5 yds or 1¾ yds 90"
Full	62 x 70	2	2 yds	1 yd	½ yd	4 yds or 2 yds 90"
Queen	78 x 93	4	2½ yds	1½ yds	¾ yd	7½ yds or 2½ yds 108" wide

** The table runner does not include outer border*

NOTE: pattern is written for the quilt size highlighted in this chart.

lucky penny

QUILT SIZE
47" X 58"

DESIGNED BY
Shea Henderson

PIECED BY
Natalie Earnheart

QUILTED BY
Mari Zullig

SAMPLE QUILT
Up Parasol by Heather Bailey for Free Spirit
Bella Solids Snow (11) by Moda

ONLINE TUTORIAL
msqc.co/luckypenny

QUILTING
Daisy Days

Quilt	Size	Charm Packs print	Charm Packs solid	Outer Border	Binding	Backing
Table Runner*	17 x 42½	(18) 5" squares or ½ pack	1	none	¼ yd	¾ yd
Throw	47 x 58	2	3	½ yd	½ yd	3¼ yds
Full	62 x 70	3	4	½ yd	½ yd	4 yds or 2 yds 90" wide

** Table runner does not have outer border.*

NOTE: pattern is written for the quilt size highlighted in this chart.

pop fly

QUILT SIZE
68″ X 82″

DESIGNED BY
Natalie Earnheart

PIECED BY
Natalie Earnheart

QUILTED BY
Amber Weeks

SAMPLE QUILT
Folklore by Lily Ashbury for Moda
Bella Solids White (98) by Moda
Bella Solids Yellow (24) by Moda

ONLINE TUTORIALS
msqc.co/popfly

QUILTING
Curls of Flowers

Quilt	Size	Jelly Rolls	Contrasting for corners	Inner Border & Sashing	Outer Border	Binding	Backing
Baby	40 x 46½	½	¼ yd	1 yd	¾ yd	½ yd	3 yds
Queen	68 x 82	1	¾ yd	2¾ yds	1¼ yds	¾ yd	5 yds or 2¼ yds 90″
King	96 x 110	2	1 yd	6 yd	1¼ yds	¾ yd	9 yds or 3¼ yds 108″

NOTE: pattern is written for the quilt size highlighted in this chart.

simple joys

QUILT SIZE
80" x 80"

DESIGNED BY
Jenny Doan

PIECED BY
Jenny Doan

QUILTED BY
Betty Bates

SAMPLE QUILT
Incarnadine by Robyn Pandolph for RJR
Cotton Supreme French Vanilla for RJR

ONLINE TUTORIALS
msqc.co/simplejoys

QUILTING
Variety

Quilt	Size	Honey Bun or yardage	Jelly Roll or strips	Outer Border	Binding	Backing
Table Runner	14 x 47	½ yd	min (8) various 2½" strips	none	¼ yd	1 yd
Throw	58 x 58	1 yd or ½ honey bun	(19) 2½" strips or ½ jelly roll	1¼ yd	½ yd	3¾ yds
Queen	80 x 80	1 honey bun	1 jelly roll	1½ yds	¾ yd	6½ yds or 2½ yds 90" wide

NOTE: pattern is written for the quilt size highlighted in this chart.

starlight, starbright

QUILT SIZE
65″ X 83″

DESIGNED BY
Jenny Doan

PIECED BY
Jenny Doan

QUILTED BY
Betty Bates

SAMPLE QUILT
Soho by Studio 8 for Quilting Treasures
Bella Solids Bleached White (98) by Moda

ONLINE TUTORIALS
msqc.co/starlight

QUILTING
Champagne Bubbles

Quilt	Size	Charm Packs	Fat Quarters for Star	Inner Border/ Background	Outer Border	Binding	Backing
Throw	47 x 65	2	2	1 yd	¾ yd	½ yd	3 yds
Full	56 x 78½	3	2	1 yd	¾ yd	½ yd	3½ yds
Queen	65 x 83	4	2	1 yd	¾ yd	¾ yd	5 yds or 2 yds 90″ wide

NOTE: pattern is written for the quilt size highlighted in this chart.

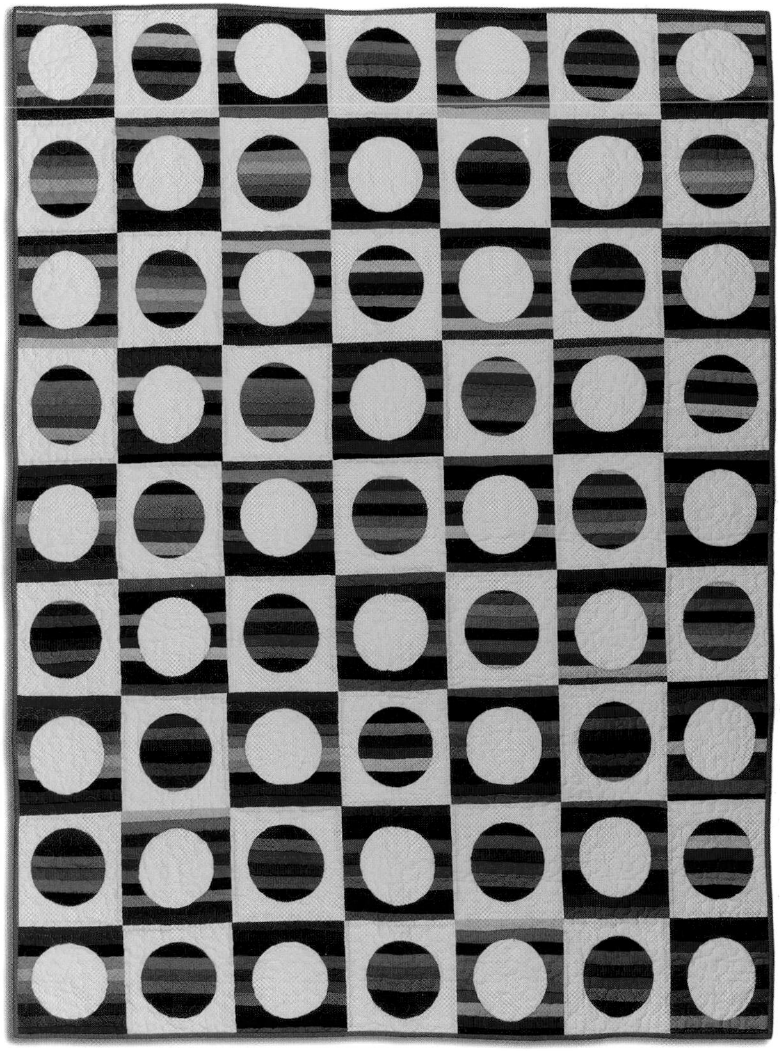

summer wishes

QUILT SIZE
71" X 91"

DESIGNED BY
Jenny Doan

PIECED BY
Cassie Nixdorf

QUILTED BY
Sherry Melton

SAMPLE QUILT
Kona Classic Collection for Robert Kaufman
Bella Solids Bleached White (98) for Moda

ONLINE TUTORIALS
msqc.co/summerwishes

QUILTING
Meander

Quilt	Size	Honey Buns	Background yardage	Binding	Backing
Table Runner or Table Topper	11 x 41 21 x 21	(10) various 1½" strips	½ yd	¼ yd	½ yd ¾ yd
Throw	51 x 61	1	2½ yds	½ yd	3¼ yds
Queen	71 x 91	2	4¾ yds	¾ yd	5½ yds or 2¼ yds 108" wide

NOTE: pattern is written for the quilt size highlighted in this chart.

sweet harvest

QUILT SIZE
61¼" X 68½"

DESIGNED BY
Jenny Doan

PIECED BY
Jenny Doan

QUILTED BY
Cassie Martin

ADDITIONAL TOOLS
MSQC Apple Core layer cake shape
Small **OR** rotating cutting mat

SAMPLE QUILT
Everything But the Kitchen Sink
by Yuko Hasegawa for RJR
Bella Solids White PDF
(97) by Moda

ONLINE TUTORIALS
msqc.co/sweetharvest

QUILT PATTERN
Meander

Quilt	Size	Layer Cakes	Background yardage	Outer Border	Binding	Backing
Table Runner*	21¾ x 58¼	(10) 10" squares	¾ yd	none	½ yd	1½ yds
Twin	54 x 75½	1	1¼ yds	1¼ yd	½ yd	3½ yds or 1¾ yds 90" wide
Full	61¼ x 68½	1	1¼ yds	1½ yd	½ yd	4 yds or 2 yds 90"
Queen	76½ x 87¾	2	1½ yds	1¾ yds	¾ yd	5½ yds or 2¾ yds 90"

** Table runner does not have outer border.*

NOTE: pattern is written for the quilt size highlighted in this chart.

tumbler bag

DESIGNED BY
Stephen Nixdorf

PIECED BY
Stephen Nixdorf

BAG
1 charm pack
¾ contrasting fabric for: bag band, strap, loop & pockets
½ yd lining

INTERFACING
2 yds Pellon shape flex 101
Fusible woven interfacing

TOOLS
MSQC 5" tumbler template

SAMPLE BAG
Hot Collective by Kaffe Fassett for Rowan/Westminster Fibers

ONLINE TUTORIALS
msqc.co/tumblerbag

general guidelines

- All seams are ¼" inch unless directions specify differently.
- Cutting instructions are given at the point when cutting is required.
- Precuts are not prewashed; therefore do not prewash other fabrics in the project
- All strips are cut WOF
- Remove all selvages
- All yardages based on 42" WOF

ACRONYMS USED

MSQC	Missouri Star Quilt Co.
RST	right sides together
WST	wrong sides together
HST	half square triangle
WOF	width of fabric
LOF	length of fabric

pre-cut glossary

CHARM PACK

1 = (42) 5" squares or ¾ yd of fabric
1 = baby
2 = crib
3 = lap
4 = twin

JELLY ROLL

1 = (42) 2½" strips cut the width of fabric or 2¾ yds of fabric
1 = a twin
2 = queen

LAYER CAKE

1 = (42) 10" squares of fabric: 2¾ yds total
1 = a twin
2 = queen

The terms charm pack, jelly roll, and layer cake are trademarked names that belong to Moda. Other companies use different terminology, but the sizes remain the same.

When we mention a precut, we are basing the pattern on a 40-42 count pack. Not all precuts have the same count, so be sure to check the count on your precut to make sure you have enough pieces to complete your project.

press seams

- Use a steam iron on the cotton setting.
- Iron the seam just as it was sewn RST. This "sets" the seam.
- With dark fabric on top, lift the dark fabric and press back.
- The seam allowance is pressed to the dark side. Some patterns may direct otherwise for certain situations.
- Follow pressing arrows in the diagrams when indicated.
- Press toward borders. Pieced borders may demand otherwise.
- Press diagonal seams open on binding to reduce bulk.

binding

- Use 2½" strips for binding.
- Sew strips end-to-end into one long strip with diagonal seams, aka plus sign method (next). Press seams open.
- Fold in half lengthwise WST and press.
- The entire length should equal the outside dimension of the quilt plus 15" - 20."

plus sign method

Diagonal seams are used when straight seams would add too much bulk.

- Lay one strip across the other as if to make a plus sign RST.
- Sew from top inside to bottom outside corners crossing the intersections of fabric as you sew. Trim excess to ¼" seam allowance.
- Press seam open.

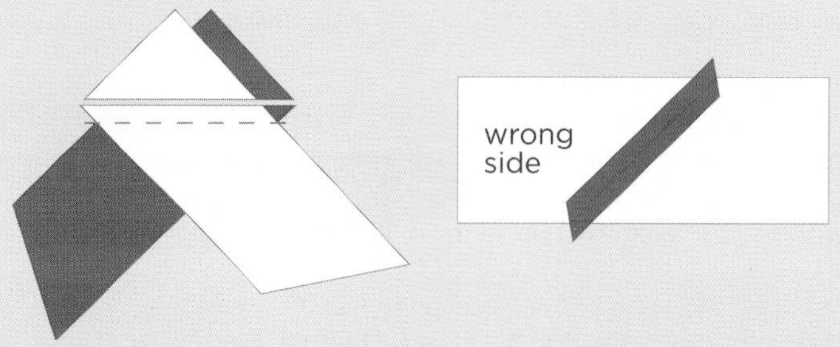

attach binding

- Match raw edges of folded binding to the quilt top edge.
- Leave a 10" tail at the beginning.
- Use a ¼" seam allowance.
- Start in the middle of a long straight side.

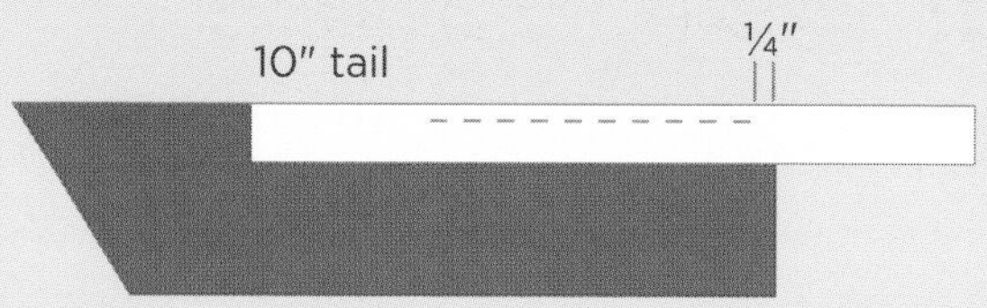

miter binding corners

- Stop sewing ¼" before the corner.
- Move the quilt out from under the pressure foot.
- Clip the threads.
- Flip the binding up at a 90˚ angle to the edge just sewn.
- Fold the binding down along the next side to be sewn.
- Align the fold to the edge of the quilt that was *just sewn*;
- Align raw edges to the side *to be sewn*.
- Begin sewing on the fold.

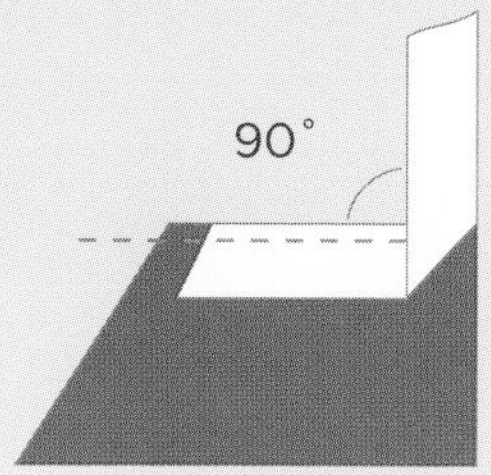

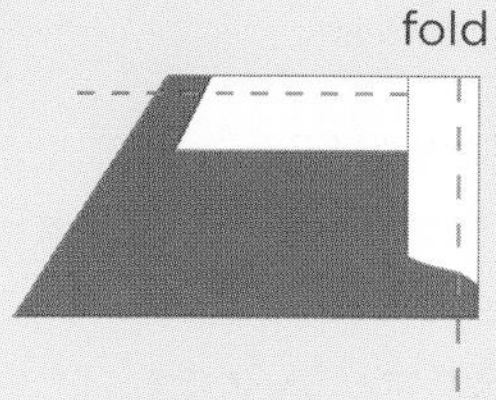

close binding

MSQC recommends **The Binding Tool** *from TQM Products to finish binding perfectly every time.*

- Stop sewing when you have 12" left to reach the start.
- Where the binding tails come together trim excess leaving only 2½" of overlap.
- It helps to pin or clip the quilt together at the two points where the binding starts and stops. This takes the pressure off of the binding tails while you work.
- Use the plus sign method to sew the two binding ends together, except this time when making the plus sign, match the edges. Using a pencil mark your sewing line since you won't be able to see where the corners intersect. Sew across.
- Trim off excess; press seam open.
- Fold in half WST and align all raw edges to the quilt top.
- Sew this last binding section to the quilt. Press.
- Turn the folded edge of the binding around to the back of the quilt and tack into place with an invisible stitch or machine stitch if you wish.

borders

- Always measure the quilt center 3 times before cutting borders.
- Start with the width and measure the top edge, middle and bottom.
- Folding the quilt in half is a quick way to find the middle.
- Take the average of those 3 measurements.
- Cut 2 border strips to that size.
- Attach one to the top; one to the bottom of the quilt.
- Position the border fabric on top as you sew. The feed dogs can act like rufflers. Having the border on top will prevent waviness and keep the quilt straight.
- Repeat this process for the side borders, measuring the length 3 times.
- Include the newly attached top and bottom borders in your measurements.
- Press to the borders.

PATCHWORK MURDER

PART 2

Disappearing Nine Patch

A JENNY DOAN MYSTERY

written by Steve Westover

Jenny shielded her eyes from the sunlight sneaking through the sheer white curtain. She rolled flat on her back and stared at the ceiling as a smile covered her face. Not even the glowing red 6:00 on the clock could dim the permacheer from her mood. It was presentation day in Oregon!

Still fully dressed Jenny pushed through the double doors into the dark interior of the suite. "MK? Are you awake?" Empty silence greeted her. "MK?" She padded through the dark toward the hide-a-bed but stopped when she knocked her shin against the coffee table. There was first a thud, then a squeal, then a... "Flabdab-bit!"

She flipped on a wall lamp. "MK?" She rushed to the neatly turned down bed where two fluffed pillows leaned against the sofa headboard. The blankets were pulled tight.

Rushing back into her room Jenny grabbed her phone from the night stand and texted MK. [Where are you?] She stared at the phone expecting an instant answer. None came but she continued staring. [Matilda Katherine!!!]

Despite the implied scolding MK didn't respond. Jenny's heart fluttered as she considered possibilities. Maybe she's at breakfast. Maybe she's coordinating with hotel staff for the presentation later. Jenny couldn't think of any reasonable explanation for MK's failure to respond. She stared at her phone for another minute and then slid it into her pocket.

Surveying the room Jenny noticed her luggage wasn't there. She opened a sliding closet door to look inside. Nothing. Jenny scowled with aggravation but then her motherly concern surfaced. She stifled a worried sigh and pulled her phone from her pocket. She stared again. Still no message.

Jenny sat on the corner of her bed and slipped on her shoes. She straightened her wrinkly blouse and sat, thinking. "Don't overreact. There's a logical explanation," she said trying to convince herself.

Rushing through the hallway, down the elevator and to the main reception desk Jenny waited...impatiently... behind a silver-haired couple. Beside her a large sign on a brass easel read

"Welcome Patchwork Quilters". Jenny glanced around the lobby without really seeing anything.

"How may I assist you?" a cheerful voice called.

Jenny leaned in close to the desk. Her words raced. "I've got a problem—two actually."

On cue the crimson vested attendant smiled. "Please tell me how I can help."

"I'm looking for my traveling companion. Maybe you've seen her." Jenny held up her phone to show the selfie she and MK had taken before take-off from Missouri.

"I'm sorry. I haven't seen her. Have you checked the dining room?"

"Not yet," Jenny confessed.

"If I see her I'll let her know you're looking for her."

Jenny considered this and then nodded in agreement. "And your second problem?" the attendant asked.

Jenny glanced back toward the mahogany pillared entrance of the dining room, anxious to go look. "My luggage. Bruno never delivered our luggage last night. I have no clothes, toothpaste...nothing." Jenny motioned over her wrinkly ensemble. "I'm making a presentation in a few hours and need to look a little fresher than this."

The attendant nodded in agreement. "You said Bruno was going to deliver your bags?"

"Yes. That's what he said."

Crow's feet formed at the corner of the attendant's eyes. "Who's Bruno?"

Jenny stared expressionless. "He's your shuttle driver." She watched the woman, expecting a glimpse of recognition but the woman's blank face mimicked Jenny's. "Good looking young man. Korean... I think."

As a guest stepped behind Jenny, all patience fled from the attendant's tone. "Ma'am, Jennifer was our driver last night. We don't have anyone named Bruno, working here." Her words made it sound like the stupidest thing she'd ever heard.

Jenny's voice rose with frustration but then lowered. "NO. I came in with other quilters on Bruno's shuttle. I checked in around 10:30 last night. Review your records. He was supposed to bring the bags to our room."

The attendant's eyes returned to her computer monitor as she dismissed Jenny. "I'm sorry I can't help you. Maybe your companion will help ease your confusion."

Jenny face flushed. "There were others who came on the same shuttle. They checked in at the same time. Ask them if I'm 'confused'."

Talking past Jenny, the attendant greeted the next guest. "How may I assist you?"

"I'd like to speak with your manager," Jenny said, unwilling to accept the brush off.

"I'll look in the dining room for my friend but I want your manager here when I return. Two minutes." Jenny strode quickly toward the Seaside Lounge, her shoes clacking on the marble

Inside, one small family sat near the back and two old men read newspapers. Jenny walked deeper inside, but no MK. Hurrying back to the front desk Jenny was pleased to see a middle aged woman waiting to greet her. A blonde bob framed the woman's smiling round face.

"Can you please help me?" Jenny asked.

"I'm the dayshift manager. How may I serve you?"

"I can't find my travel companion or my luggage. She," Jenny said pointing to the attendant, "said you don't have a shuttle driver named Bruno. Is that true?"

"That's true."

"This is crazy." When she noticed the manager's look of pity Jenny amended her statement. "This is crazy. I'm not crazy. I know he said his name was Bruno. It didn't fit so I remembered. Other guests checked in at the same time. Can you please ask them if they received their luggage? Maybe mine was delivered to another room by mistake," Jenny suggested.

The manager studied Jenny and then nodded in consigned agreement. "It's early, but let me ring the other rooms."

"Thank you."

Behind the counter, the manager typed quickly and then jotted notes on a pad. She called the first room, apologized for the earliness of the call and asked about their luggage. The manager frowned. "Thank you. We will get to the bottom of this."

"No luggage?" Jenny asked.

The manager didn't answer because she was already dialing the next room. The conversation was identical. She made notes and then called another room. No answer. She called the final room. No answer. When the manager turned to whisper in the attendant's ear Jenny leaned across the desk to peak at the notepad. It was too quick to read the manager's scribbles, but she committed two room numbers to memory: 332 and 409. The attendant rushed away.

"There's nothing to worry about," the manager said nervously.

"Except that you may have a thief impersonating hotel staff. Other than that, no worries at all." Jenny paused and looked around anxiously. "Please call me when you find my bags. I do have a presentation at 11:00."

"Yes, of course," the manager said.

The hike to room 332 felt even longer than the eternal elevator ride. Jenny knocked on the door, soft at first, but then harder when no one answered. Her heart thumped in her chest as she gulped down her anxiety. She listened and then knocked again. There was a rustle from deep inside. When the door opened, a sixty-something with a powerful red dye job stood bleary-eyed in a white Harrington robe.

"I'm sorry to bother you," Jenny said, "but were you on the shuttle from the airport with me last night?"

The woman's glare pierced Jenny but then softened as she nodded. "Yes."

"Was there a Korean driver named Bruno?"

The woman's forehead creased with concentration as if Jenny had asked her to piece a Missouri Star with just her toes. "Yeah, weird name for an Asian man."

"Was your luggage delivered to your room?" Jenny asked.

The woman sneered and then unloaded. Jenny got the message fast. A big "NO".

"Thank you for your time," Jenny said. Before the woman could continue her rant Jenny rounded a corner back toward the bank of elevators.

The door to room 409 looked like every other door in the hotel with one notable exception; it was propped open by the bolt lever at eye level. A copy of the Oregonian lay neatly on the floor. Jenny leaned toward the crack, listened for a moment and then knocked. She heard something that sounded like a tussle and then a thud. She knocked again.

"Hello," she called. No one responded and the sounds of movement inside hushed. Turning, she looked down the long hallway. A father and a young girl entered a room at the far end of the corridor leaving Jenny alone in the hallway.

Jenny's heart beat against her ribcage with the rhythm of a bass drum. "I'm coming in," she said as pleasantly and calmly a she could manage but she could hear the quaver in her voice. "It's just me. Nothing to be worried about. I'm a nice person," she said in a sing-song tone.

The door pushed inward but stopped with a metallic clank. After another quick peek down the hall Jenny pushed the door in farther and entered, her eyes darting around the room. She removed the bolt that had been propping the door open and then backed against the door, shutting it tight as she exhaled heavily.

"Hello," she repeated as she pushed her way past a tall brass luggage carrier. "Is anyone here?" she asked, her voice barely a whisper.

With both layers of curtains drawn the dark room felt claustrophobic. Jenny swallowed as her hand searched the wall for a switch. When the light flickered on she exhaled with relief...until she saw the queen size beds stacked with suitcases. Except for one hot pink leopard print bag, the luggage appeared ordinary. She moved closer towards the center of the beds to examine the luggage tags, expecting to find hers and MK's, but she tripped and fell forward. Bracing herself on the corner of the bed she looked at a crumpled duvet covering a lump on the floor. A man's sneaker protruded from the cover. Jenny's hands shot to her mouth to muffle her shriek. She stared at the lump while her mouth gaped open. She tapped the sneaker with her shoe.

The lump remained still without even a hint of annoyance that someone dared kick it. No breathing. No movement of any kind. Jenny's mouth sagged to accommodate her rapid breathing as she bent over and pinched the duvet fabric between her thumb and forefinger. She pulled the cover back, first revealing short black hair and then Bruno's glassy eyes staring past her. Gray duct tape covered his mouth. Dropping the cover back over Bruno's face Jenny screamed and scurried around the bed toward the door.

Grabbing the phone from her pocket Jenny started to dial but stopped and screamed again when she felt a hand pull at her shoulder. Jenny reeled around to see MK's tear stained face. Jenny's and MK's shoulders heaved in cadence. She clutched MK to her. "MK, what are you doing here?" Jenny asked, her voice shaking.

MK opened her mouth to answer but for a full minute only sobs came out. Then she forced her words between her heaving cries. "I didn't do it, Jenny. I swear. I didn't. I can explain."

Jenny grabbed MK's shoulders and nodded fervently. "I believe you." She wrapped an arm tightly around her niece and led her from the room.

With their backs against the hallway wall opposite room 409 Jenny and MK sat with their arms wrapped around each other. "What's going to happen?" MK asked between sniffles.

"I don't know," Jenny said, shaking her head. "Don't worry. It's my turn to take care of you." She squeezed MK tight and then dialed 911. The sound of the operator's voice chilled her as the gravity of the situation rested upon her like Bruno's duvet shroud.

Jenny squeezed MK's shoulder and then kissed her on the forehead. "I'll figure this out, MK. I'll take care of everything," Jenny promised.